New
Directions in
African
Architecture

NEW DIRECTIONS IN ARCHITECTURE

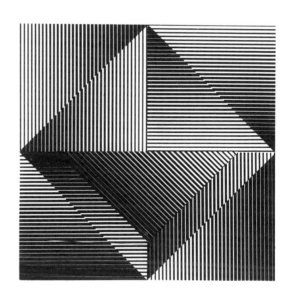

UDO KULTERMANN

NEW DIRECTIONS

IN

AFRICAN

ARCHITECTURE

GEORGE BRAZILLER   NEW YORK

Translated by John Maass

CONTENTS

12/21/76- Published -$5.95

FOREWORD

In contrast to numerous surveys of the contemporary architecture of other continents, there have been few devoted to Africa. There are studies of tropical architecture as well as books which focus on individual regions, but comprehensive surveys of Africa's architecture have rarely been undertaken—perhaps because of the difficulties posed by so diverse and diffuse a subject. My book, *New Architecture in Africa* (1963), was an initial attempt in this direction, but I could account for only a few native architects and two of these were still strongly influenced by the French or British tradition. Such was the situation in 1960.

The present book, dealing with the current scene, allows for a different emphasis, one which makes it possible to assign a majority of illustrations to buildings by native architects. Recent ideas developed by Europeans living in Africa are included as cornerstones in the creation of an indigenous and appropriate architecture for the continent.

I have tried to show tendencies which are clearly evident today as well as those which point to the future, and to integrate the contributions of African architects with those of non-Africans. The best way to accomplish this task was to organize the subject according to types of buildings which, though handled differently from region to region, still permit some basis of comparison.

My sincere thanks are due to all the architects who assisted me on my travels in North, West, and South Africa. I am particularly grateful to the architects Godwin and Hopwood, Oluwole Olumuyiwa, A. Ifeanyi Ekwueme, and S. I. Kola-Bankole in Lagos, Julian Elliott in Capetown, Elie Azagury and Jean-François Zevaco in Casablanca, H. Richard Hughes in Nairobi, Kenneth Scott in Accra, Olivier-Clement Cacoub in Tunis, Peer Abben in Honolulu, E. Maxwell Fry, Jane Drew, Denys Lasdun, and Lindsay Drake in London, Renato Severini in Rome, and José Ravelomanantsoa, Jean Rafamatanantsoa, and Jean Rabemanantsoa in Tananarive. I received further valuable insights from the publications of Amancio d'Alpoim Guedes in Lourenço Marques, Julian Beinart in Johannesburg, John Lloyd in Kumasi, and Alan Vaughan-Richards in Lagos. In their writings African architecture is viewed in an international context, and they rightly point out that this seemingly underdeveloped continent offers reserve powers for the universal culture which is needed today.

INTRODUCTION

Contemporary architecture in Africa is too diverse, too heterogeneous, even too contradictory, to be readily defined or categorized. It includes building traditions which go back thousands of years, and construction techniques recently imported from Europe and America. Huts made of plant materials; structures of colonial origin; first attempts at indigenous architecture; building forms of the Stone Age, the early Christian era, the feudal period, and the twentieth century —all these are to be found side by side. It is not yet possible to speak of a truly African architecture.

It must be remembered that, with a few earlier exceptions, hardly a decade has passed since the political emancipation of African colonies. No one could have foreseen how rapidly and radically this emancipation would proceed. Inevitably, independence unleashed internal struggles for power in the new states. Then, too, the frontiers of these states have no national or ethnic bases; they originated for the most part through accidents of the colonial period.

As a result, there is no common culture within regions or countries. If such a culture is to arise, it must be newly constituted, and in Africa this is a formidable task. Responsibility for the creation of an African culture, as for African politics, is still in the hands of the few. Most still cling to the older tribal tradition which is often in opposition to the officially proclaimed culture; they are seldom in a position even to recognize that a new will is needed. For example, in Nigeria, the most highly developed state of black Africa, the percentage of college-educated citizens in 1958, two years before independence, was only 0.025 percent. In the Congo, which is as large as Western Europe, in the independence year of 1960 there was a total of eight college-educated black citizens.

Tribal ways of thinking which once played an important role can perhaps be revitalized on a new basis, though not without danger. The continued struggle of Biafra for secession from Nigeria, for example, has demonstrated that tribalism can create tragic divisions with an inevitable impact on the culture of a country. As Fritz Schatten wrote in 1961 in *Afrika—Schwarz oder Rot?* (Africa—Black or Red?): "A whole millennium stands between the national dream of the few and the inertia of the many; wherever Africa attempts to bridge the enormous gap between the day before yesterday and the day after tomorrow, the difficulty and danger of this leap becomes quickly evident."

It is characteristic of contemporary African culture that maximum opportunities exist with little potential for their realization. Without undue pessimism it can be said that after the great advances of the early sixties, political development is regressive. The same holds true for architecture, which is linked inseparably to social and political conditions. Only scattered results have materialized after the high hopes and expectations of the early sixties which we can now examine much more soberly.

Shortly after 1960, Africans wanted to replace foreign architects, technicians, and specialists with native personnel as quickly as possible. Today, when a project is initiated and financed with calm deliberation, optimal performance and not the color of a man's skin is the determinant. Prominent commissions like the universities of Zambia at Lusaka (Julian Elliott) or Cape Coast in Ghana (COMTEC) were almost entirely planned and executed by white men. The clients in both cases were black. This is symptomatic of the more flexible attitude which evolved toward the end of the sixties.

An architecture based on European and American models fails to meet the needs of the new African states, but the revived tribal spirit has not provided workable alternatives. A combination is needed: the newly activated African tradition, which is still largely unconscious, and the latest technical and construction methods from abroad. Before this can happen, however, an identification with tradition must be reawakened in Africans themselves. Up to now this effort has been made almost entirely by Europeans, who naturally approach it with European standards. The valid tradition of the African must be fundamentally differentiated from European culture and revived as such.

The character of the African is based upon dynamics which are wholly fulfilled in the present rather than in striving to create eternal values. For the African, life itself, the immediate self, and the moment are important. This explains the fundamental differences of tradition and of the surviving architectural monuments. Cultures whose monuments are built of perishable materials imply the concept of perishability; they are much more open to the forces and methods of tradition than cultures which strive to create monuments for eternity, and must live with buildings constructed from relatively indestructible materials.

Today architecture can no longer be understood as a fixed, static reality. It grows out of time and space; it takes form in motion and becoming. We realize that social development is dynamic, and that the task of the architect changes according to the times. In the same way, architecture must be understood as a constant renewal. From this viewpoint the consideration of ancient African architecture is particularly important, and has special significance for the architecture now emerging. Will young architects in Africa—African or non-

African—be able to establish a link with this old tradition? If so, what will the results look like? Are these newly seen and newly appreciated models beginning to affect African architecture? Or will building techniques which are adapted only superficially to the local conditions of the capitals of the independent states prevail? Here tradition could be a needed corrective. But, first, tradition would again have to be accepted as the natural heritage, rather than as a thing of the past.

Among the most basic building forms of man are the cave dwellings; these exist in several places at the edge of the desert in southern Tunisia. The principal place, already open to tourists, is the village of Old-Matmata which is still wholly inhabited. The cave as a dwelling also plays an important part in East Africa. Cave dwellings similar to those in southern Tunisia have been found in use by the Agau peoples of northern Ethiopia. It may be considered certain that underground dwellings were once widespread throughout the entire Sahara region and remnants are still found in southern Morocco. It is no coincidence that North African cave dwellings have features in common with cellars of the ancient Sudan, at the southern edge of the Sahara. Leo Frobenius already noted these similarities in his book *Monumenta Africana* and related them to tombs of the ancient Sudan.

Matmata lies in a valley about fifty kilometers southwest of the Gabes oasis; it can be reached over a mountain road with many bends and grades. As seen from above, the houses resemble huge open molehills (*Figs. 1–2*). The rooms have been hollowed out of firm clay soil. No other material has been used, at least not in the original type. A canyon-like entry, open to the sky, leads to the front door. From there, a passageway runs underground into what is now often used as a stable, and then into an open courtyard which is the center of the house. From the courtyard, shaftlike rooms at different levels lead underground; they are arranged in a star-shaped layout and contain a kitchen, a storeroom for supplies, rooms for sleeping and eating, and a toilet. Since they receive light only from the courtyard opening they lie in semidarkness. They have a regular though not rectangular design and were probably constructed by grinding the clay soil with pointed tools.

These building forms probably date back to prehistoric times and were perhaps later rediscovered by the Berbers. Leo Frobenius wrote in 1912 that, "Unless all evidence is deceptive, prehistoric men in many places lived in caves and underground pits; these go back so far that we must consider them the original building forms."

Another tradition can be traced in the urban cultures of West Africa. The historian Jacob Egharevba has written about the history of his native city of Benin, Nigeria, relating that the kingdom of Benin was founded over a thousand years ago by people who came from Egypt. The city was almost entirely destroyed by fire in 1897, but we know of its brilliance and grandeur from historical accounts. These

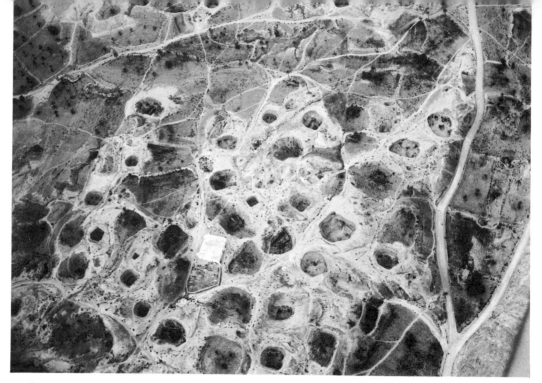

1. *Cave dwellings at Matmata, Tunisia, airview.*

2. *Plan of a cave dwelling, Matmata, Tunisia.*

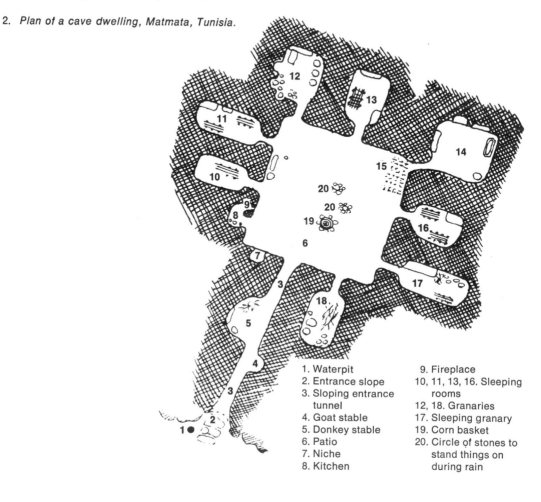

1. Waterpit
2. Entrance slope
3. Sloping entrance tunnel
4. Goat stable
5. Donkey stable
6. Patio
7. Niche
8. Kitchen
9. Fireplace
10, 11, 13, 16. Sleeping rooms
12, 18. Granaries
17. Sleeping granary
19. Corn basket
20. Circle of stones to stand things on during rain

descriptions state that Benin was enclosed by a wall with seven gates (*Fig. 3*). The city itself was divided in two by a broad street; the king resided in the smaller, southwestern section along with the court and the dignitaries, the city chiefs lived in the larger section (*Fig. 4*). Both parts of the city were divided into over forty districts, each having a different obligation toward the king according to the occupation of its inhabitants. Within these districts priests, doctors, court officials, metalsmiths, ivory carvers, to name but a few, lived in separate communities, as was the practice in the cities of medieval Europe.

When the Portuguese arrived in Benin around 1500, they found a city-state which was "a nautical mile long from gate to gate"; the inhabitants were prosperous and experienced in metalworking. In 1668, the Dutchman Dapper reported that:

> The city has thirty quite straight streets. Each is about thirty-six meters wide with many broad though somewhat narrower cross streets running into them. The houses stand along orderly streets, close to each other as in Europe, decorated with gables and steps, and roofed with palm and banana leaves. Though not very high, they are usually large with long corridors inside, especially in the houses of noblemen. These houses have many rooms whose walls are made of reddish clay which they know how to smooth with washing and scouring so that the walls gleam like a mirror.

Dapper also reported that the palace district of Benin was as large as the Dutch city of Haarlem, and that the galleries in the district were as large as the Stock Exchange of Amsterdam. There was also a tower between eighteen and twenty-one meters high, with a great copper snake on top. Benin was not an isolated example of a cosmopolitan culture: others in Yorubaland—Ibadan, Kano (*Fig. 5*), and Lagos—continue to live on as great cities.

Ancient African architecture was by no means limited to structures made out of wood, plants, clay, and termite earth. Throughout East Africa there were cities built of stone which today count among the world's greatest architectural achievements. The East African coastal cities built before the fifteenth century, having maritime connections as far as China, resembled the rich ports of southern Europe, or India. They had white terraces, tall houses, and paved quays, and were ringed by strong walls and crowned by palaces and fortresses.

The castles of Zimbabwe (in present Rhodesia) are the culmination of ancient East African architecture. For a long time, attempts were made to link the culture evidenced in these ruins to foreign immigrants, but it is fairly clear that Zimbabwe ("the stone house") had a decidedly African tradition. In his book *Da Asia* (c. 1530), João de Barros described the castles:

A. The house for ye old and young Queens.
B. The yard of ye Royall court.
C. The gate of said court.
D. The Palace of ye Kings court.
E. The Kings progres which het Rideth once a year.
F. His nobles & kindred on horsback.
G. The musicians playing after the King.
H. The fools & Dwarfs.
I. The players before ye King & Tame Leopards.

De Stadt
BENI
The City
BENIN

A . t'Vrouwen timmer of Huys van de Oude
    en Ionge Koninginne .
B . Wal van het Koninglÿcke Hof .
C . De Poort des zelven Hofs .
D . Paleisen des Konings Hofs .
E . Staesi hoe de Koning een mael
    S'Iaers Vitrydt .
F . Syn Adel en Bloetvrienden te Paert .
G . Speelders achter den Koning .
H . Gekken en Dwergen .
I . Speelders voor den Koning met
    tamme Tygers .

3. *Benin City, Nigeria.*

In the center of a plain lies a square fortress, very well built, within and without, of cut stones and of wonderful size. There is no lime to be seen in the joints. The wall is more than three meters wide but the height does not match the width. Above the portal is an inscription which learned Moorish merchants who were there could not read, nor could they determine the character of the inscription. Around this building, on various hills, are other buildings like the first, executed in stone without lime. Inside stands a tower of more than thirteen meters height. The natives call all these buildings Zimbabwe which means residence.

The German explorer Carl Mauch, who was the first to view these ruins again about one hundred years ago, believed Zimbabwe was

4. *Benin City and the royal palace, Nigeria, plan.*

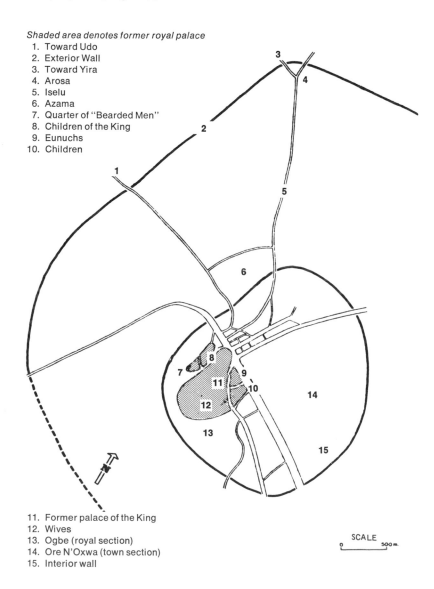

Shaded area denotes former royal palace
1. Toward Udo
2. Exterior Wall
3. Toward Yira
4. Arosa
5. Iselu
6. Azama
7. Quarter of "Bearded Men"
8. Children of the King
9. Eunuchs
10. Children

11. Former palace of the King
12. Wives
13. Ogbe (royal section)
14. Ore N'Oxwa (town section)
15. Interior wall

SCALE
0   500 m.

the biblical country known as Ophir—the source of gold for King Solomon's empire. He thought that the "acropolis" of Zimbabwe was a copy of the king's temple and that the ruin lying in the plain below was modeled after the palace in which the Queen of Sheba stayed during her visit to the king. Although these theories have been disproven, Mauch's account (written in 1871) remains a fascinating document. He describes his first impressions of the site:

> The ruin consists of two parts: the remnants of one were on top of a high, isolated hill; those of the other, about a kilometer to the south, separated by a small sandfilled valley. The outer wall of the mountain ruin is particularly noteworthy; it apparently served as a fortification and is built with great daring on the rounded edge of an eighteen-meter-high rocky mass. Inside, thinner walls enclose a rectangular, elongated room which is bordered by a curved wall on the west side. The walls are all built without

5. *Kano, Nigeria, airview.*

mortar; the thinner walls of the inner building have almost entirely fallen so that it was difficult to make one's way over the
piles of loose debris, overgrown with sizeable trees, underbrush
and bushlike nettles. From the inner room, toward the summit of
the rock, led several covered ways, probably into crevices and
chasms, perhaps also into larger underground rooms of appar-
ently later origin and walled up by Kaffirs. The entire western
slope of the hill was covered with debris that suggested a ter-
raced layout.

This account of the Zimbabwe acropolis is followed by a de-
scription of the second great ruin, the so-called elliptical building
(*Figs. 6–7*). The natives gave its name to Mauch as *Munka huru,*
"House of the Great Woman." Mauch wrote that:

> The other ruin in the plain presents a great roundel with a wall
> eight meters high, four meters thick at the base, and two meters
> thick at the top. The only entrance appears to have been on the
> side facing the mountain [acropolis]. In the interior, the thinner
> walls lose themselves in a curving labyrinth [*Fig. 8*]. Traces
> show that the rooms seem to have been used at times as a refuge
> by pursued natives. The most curious feature with the roundel,
> opposite the entrance, was a tower about ten meters high; the
> heap of debris at the base of this tapering cone hid any entrance
> from view. I climbed on a creeper plant to the top which had a
> diameter of two meters. I uncovered a few layers of stones with-
> out being able to see any hollow inside. Ruins of large buildings
> were also on the side of the roundel toward the mountain.

Mauch considered the ruins of Zimbabwe fascinating architectural documents but was not able to value them as monuments of
African architecture. It was Leo Frobenius who placed them within
Africa's cultural history, after the British archaeologist Caton-
Thompson had completed the basic studies. Frobenius was able to
connect the visible ruins with the extensive underground shafts and
mines which produced Zimbabwe's wealth, and to place the city in
relation to the great settlements in Engaruka and Mapungubwe as
one of the principal sites of a lost African culture.

The castles of Zimbabwe, only occasionally visited by tourists,
lie in a beautiful Rhodesian landscape. The curving walls and passages have suggested that the city was a labyrinth designed for a
cult (the passages would have served for ritual dances). Father Sche-
besta believed that the elliptical building was the funerary temple of
a sun king. The most likely theory is that the site was intended for
refuge and defense. This could apply not only to the acropolis, whose
high location is ideal for defense, but also to the elliptical building
(or temple). The latter has, in part, three rings of walls and extends
through smaller buildings toward the acropolis. The layout, which is
curved throughout, recalls the *kraals* (huts grouped in a compound)

6. *Zimbabwe, elliptical building.*

7. *Zimbabwe, elliptical building, interior wall.*

8. *Zimbabwe, elliptical building, conical tower, interior.*

still existing in the area. Zimbabwe was probably a court center of religious and economic significance with far-ranging connections. It is linked to the East African traditions of stone buildings on hills and to the terrace cultures. Together they testify to a rich flowering that began in the sixth century and seems to have perished in the eighteenth century. The numerous ruins were then forgotten and have come into view again only in recent years.

Today's viewer is fascinated by the magnificent architectural achievement. The acropolis consists of various wall and passage systems, strongly differentiated in height and built into the rock— technique and nature have become inseparable. We are facing a "total" architecture in the sense defined by Walter Gropius: master-pieces of organic building which are comparable to the works of major twentieth-century architects.

All of these ancient African building forms, determined by cli-matic, economic, religious, and social conditions, should be rec-ognized as the historical basis for developing a modern African architecture. Tradition, however, can live only when it is directly related to the goals of the present, and can be effective only when it is suitable for today's pressing needs. It is not possible simply to apply traditional building materials, forms, and types to a building program which demands new means. Clay, for example, cannot be successfully used to build a hospital, as has been tried in South Africa; this would only be a romanticization of the past. It is essential to recognize the greatly changed social conditions of the present and to create new designs based on inexpensive building materials, combining the old (clay, wood, and stone) with the new (concrete, aluminum, and iron). The spirit of the past must be revived, renewed, and accommodated to the needs of the present.

The social changes which proceed with unheard of rapidity are largely determined by urbanization. An endless stream of people pours from the bush villages into the great cities where industry offers work. Édea in Cameroon, Fria in Guinea, and Katanga in the Republic of the Congo stand beside the great cities of Johannesburg, Salisbury, Leopoldville, Cairo, Algiers, Casablanca, Tunis, or Nairobi as new industrial centers. The central problems of these cities are the same as those which face many other cities around the world, and can indeed be regarded as the unsolved problems of society in general: the shelters of the poor, for instance, in the "temporary" districts around the core of the great cities. They are mostly made of the waste material of Western civilization—corrugated iron, wood, tin cans, textiles, leaves, and clay. Buildings of this kind have been put up by the millions in Africa, and—though intended for temporary use—have become permanent housing: the bidonvilles, the tin-can towns, and similar shanties at the edges of urban centers stand as testimony. The appearance of most African cities today is determined by these build-ings.

However, this aesthetically worthless architecture should not be underestimated. The African's characteristic inclination to community living has made many of these slums into lively townships, thus presenting a double contrast to numerous state-planned and mechanically executed housing developments. Discussions about housing densities and the renewal of city cores still suffer from the unresolved conflict of planning in the abstract versus the actual desires of people.

Any consideration of African architecture must, above all, take into account that the building forms in various parts of the continent are determined by the climate (*cf. Figs. 9–10*). The varying and interacting conditions of climate—including the effects of heat, humidity, wind and, vegetation—have created such geographic extremes as desert, steppe, and primeval forest, often close to each other. For example, in North Africa—especially in Morocco—the architectural solutions required in this very hot, dry climate differ from those in the hot but humid climate of West Africa—mainly Nigeria—which demand ventilation. Various parts of East Africa, Kenya, and the Republic of South Africa, have a moderate climate, and the architecture often

9. *The Sahara.*

resembles the Mediterranean style of southern Europe or the American South. African architecture can be planned correctly only with attention to these very different regional conditions.

In tropical regions, the attitude toward air-conditioning is ambivalent. In most office and administrative buildings in Central Africa, air-conditioning provides insulation from outside temperatures which would otherwise make the building of doubtful use. But entering such a building in a tropical city causes a physical shock, and it requires considerable time to adjust to the cool, dry climate of the interior. Air-conditioning is not a universal panacea; its installation must be carefully considered and specially adapted to the micro-climate, which changes in the course of a day; interior and exterior spaces should be connected by a gradual transition of temperature, with only a few degrees of difference. Young West African architects therefore prefer the traditional and often effective cross ventilation of colonial architecture to the technical difficulties and expense of air-conditioning. To be successful, architecture in Africa needs to meet both the programmatic requirements of the building and regional building traditions. To date, this twin goal has not been widely achieved.

10. *The Oasis.*

BUILDINGS

Educational

IT is no accident that the most significant architectural achievements in Africa are to be found among educational buildings. The basic schooling of the African—as well as the education of his teachers— ranks before all economic, political, military, and other considerations. Elementary and technical schools, teachers' colleges, and universities are thus the primary tasks of building in the new nations.

Universities and Colleges

Universities existed in Africa even before the great movement toward independence. There are, for example, the institutions founded by Englishmen at Ibadan, Nigeria, the technical college (since converted into a university) at Kumasi, Ghana, and Makerere College in Uganda. Islamic institutions of higher learning in North Africa and the universities in the Republic of South Africa have an even older tradition.

The University College at Ibadan, by E. Maxwell Fry and Jane Drew, is one of the major educational structures on the continent. The huge, sprawling campus features buildings with pierced walls, adapted to the West African climate and derived from the Yoruba tradition of cross ventilation. The library is a long four-story building which provides maximum shade and ventilation. The social facilities on the campus, such as the dining hall (covered by a large dome with open sides), or the student residences within the complex, follow the same principles. The former Kumasi College of Technology is of equal importance, having an extensive campus with typical student housing and various colleges in the British tradition of Oxford and Cambridge. The Englishman James Cubitt, who designed several lecture halls and the laboratory building at Kumasi, paid special attention to the regional climate (*Fig. 11*).

Other college complexes in this part of Africa are by Frank Rutter, who designed the student housing of Fourah Bay University in Freetown, Sierra Leone; by the Architects' Co-Partnership, which built living quarters for the employees of Lagos University; by the African A. Ifeanyi Ekwueme, who designed the laboratory building for St. Gregory's College in Nigeria (*Fig. 12*); and by Oluwole Olumuyiwa who designed the College of Engineering in Ibadan (*Fig. 13*); as well as by S. I. Kola-Bankole who built the new Botany Laboratory for the University of Ibadan (*Fig. 14*). Since 1966 the Italian firm COMTEC,

11. *James Cubitt: Engineering Building, Kumasi University, Ghana.*

12. *A. Ifeanyi Ekwueme: Laboratory Building, St. Gregory's College, Lagos, Nigeria.*

13. *Oluwole Olumuyiwa: College of Engineering, Ibadan, Nigeria.*

14. *S. I. Kola-Bankole: New Botany Laboratory, University of Ibadan, Nigeria.*

under its chief architect, Renato Severini, has undertaken the master plan for the University College of Science and Education at Cape Coast, Ghana. The social and cultural centers of this university, reminiscent of Le Corbusier's late work, set a high standard of modern design for Africa (*Figs. 15–16*). Even though these ideas stem from foreign architects, they are far more convincing than most attempts made by Africans to combine their own tradition with technical influences from abroad.

The most important project of this kind on the continent is the planning and building of the University of Zambia in Lusaka, which has been entrusted to a British architect, Julian Elliott. After careful studies in Europe and America Elliott, with the planner Anthony

15. *COMTEC (Renato Severini, chief architect): Cultural Center, University of Cape Coast, Ghana, model, 1966—*

16. *COMTEC (Renato Severini, chief architect): Social Center, University of Cape Coast, Ghana.*

Chitty and the chief architect Douglas Yetter, began to formulate a new concept of a university. The evolution of the project from the first designs in 1965 to the present shows the convincing progress of these efforts. On two parallel tracts, the academic buildings face the administrative and recreational facilities (*Fig. 17*). These are connected by a meeting hall in the student center, by dining rooms, and by the central library. The two parallel units can be extended and adapted to meet new demands. The first step toward a university designed exclusively by African architects is the project for University City in Tananarive, the Malagasy Republic, by the architects José Ravelomanantsoa, Jean Ratamatanantsoa, and Jean Rabemanantsoa (*Fig. 18*).

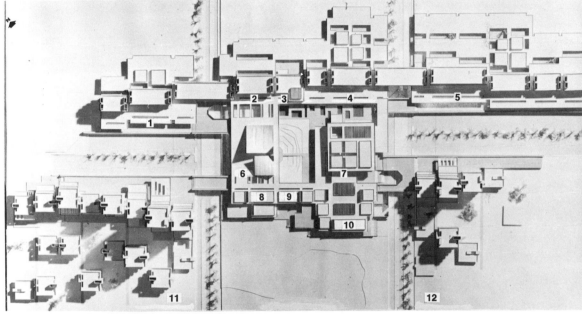

1. Schools of Education and Administration
2. African Studies Center
3. University Offices
4. School of Humanities
5. School of Natural Sciences
6. Assembly Hall
7. Library
8. Student Center
9. Bookshop
10. Dining Hall
11. Northwest Residential Group
12. Southeast Residential Group

17. *Julian Elliott: University of Zambia, Lusaka, Zambia, view of model.*

18. *José Ravelomanantsoa, Jean Ratamatanantsoa, and Jean Rabemanantsoa: Project University City, Tananarive, the Malagasy Republic, model.*

Teachers' Colleges

James Cubitt's design for a teachers' college in Secondi, Ghana, possesses a form appropriate to the region while meeting the needs of the program (*Fig. 19*). Fry Drew Partners built the teachers' college at Kano, in northern Nigeria. Another institution of this type is the Higher Teacher Training College in Bamako, Mali, which was assigned to the American firm TAC (The Architects' Collaborative) in 1966.

The Centres Reéducations are a special type of educational housing developed by the Moroccan architect Jean-François Zevaco at Tit-Mellil and Ben-Slimane. These are derived unmistakably from the French tradition but are distinguished by a greater freedom and boldness of shape (*Fig. 20*). The buildings at Ben-Slimane (erected in 1955, 1959, and 1961) form a radial multiwing complex—tied together by passages; here the relationship of the pavilion-like units is especially appropriate. The structure at Tit-Mellil, built in three stages 1952, 1955, and 1959), has a boldly projecting form in axis with the main lecture hall in the center (*Figs. 20–21*). The diagonal forms, set on a not entirely resolved base, are an effective architectural solution, the kind which has contributed to the revaluation of once misunderstood African needs.

19. *James Cubitt: Teachers' Training College and Secondary School, Secondi, Ghana.*

20. *Jean-François Zevaco: Reeducation Center, Tit-Mellil, Morocco.*

21. *Jean-François Zevaco: Reeducation Center, Tit-Mellil, Morocco, model.*

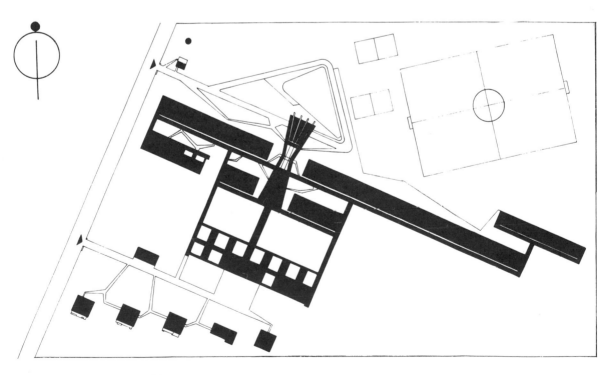

The Northern Police College in Kaduna, northern Nigeria, by Godwin and Hopwood, has a rectangular layout with classrooms, meeting hall, and mosque. Here, too, the structure is determined by the typically West African pierced "breathing" walls (*Fig. 22*).

Elementary Schools

Although elementary schools play a crucial role in the education of African children, architectural solutions can come about only in those communities which have recognized the need for an educated citizenry and therefore place a high value on schools. This is essentially the case in Morocco and Algeria, and in the large West African cities like Lagos and Ibadan.

E. Maxwell Fry, long active on the continent, designed schools for some parts of West Africa more than twenty years ago: in Apowa, Ghana, he built a school for boys and in Aburi, one for girls. Godwin and Hopwood's Okesuna Municipal School in Lagos is a large glass-walled complex in the center of the city. At their special school for the blind and the deaf in Lagos Surulere, residences for the staff were incorporated into the scheme. The Africans A. Ifeanyi Ekwueme and Oluwole Olumuyiwa have also designed schools in or near Lagos, including the United Christian Commercial Secondary School (*Fig. 23*), and a number of elementary schools (*Figs. 24–25*). In Cameroon, Olaf Jacobsen designed the school at Yaoundé. The use of large parallel tracts on a sloping site, connected by a central unit, is a practical prototype for Central Africa. In Ethiopia, Emperor Haile Selassie's model school, the First Elementary School in Addis Ababa, achieves its appealing quality through the combined use of native materials and traditional building methods.

Africa's most important schools were built in Morocco. Moroccans trained in France, like Jean-François Zevaco and Elie Azagury, and younger French-influenced architects like Castelneau and Tastemain, did exemplary work. Zevaco designed schools in Casablanca and Quarzazate, a second large school complex in Agadir, and the Groupe Scolaire in Agadir-Talborjt (*Figs. 26–30*). Zevaco treats concrete rhythmically though somewhat repetitively, but he knows how to mold architecture into a sculptured form. Elie Azagury's schools are less dramatic but more functional than Zevaco's works. This is especially true of his center in Casablanca, where he developed simple, basic shapes. The African architects José Ravelomanantsoa and Jean Rabemanantsoa designed the school complex at Anosy, in the Malagasy Republic (*Fig. 31*).

Government

Government architecture—both state and municipal—is secondary to school construction. However, the emancipated nations, stamped by a growing nationalism, require administrative, legislative, and

22. *John Godwin and Gillian Hopwood: Northern Police College, Kaduna, Nigeria, 1963.*

23. *A. Ifeanyi Ekwueme: United Christian Commercial Secondary School, Apapa, Lagos, Nigeria, view from corridor toward library.*

24. *Oluwole Olumuyiwa: Elementary School, Lagos, Nigeria.*

25. *Oluwole Olumuyiwa: Elementary School, Lagos, Nigeria.*

judicial buildings to house the workings of new government. Similarly, municipalities must create city halls and other civic facilities. Sometimes it is possible for the new government to take over and adapt buildings left by colonial predecessors. In Senegal, the Palace of the Grand Counsel, designed by the French architects Badani and Roux Dorlut, was originally built as an administrative center of French colonial power in West Africa. It now serves as the parliament of the independent state although the character of the building does not reflect the democratic spirit of a legislative body but rather symbolizes the power and authority of French colonialism.

26. *Jean-François Zevaco: Groupe Scolaire, Casablanca, Morocco.*

27. Jean-François Zevaco: Groupe Scolaire, Agadir-Talborjt, Morocco.

28. Jean-François Zevaco: Groupe Scolaire, Agadir, Morocco, 1966.

29. *Jean-François Zevaco: School, Quarzazate, Morocco, 1966.*

30. *Jean-François Zevaco: School, Quarzazate, Morocco, 1966.*

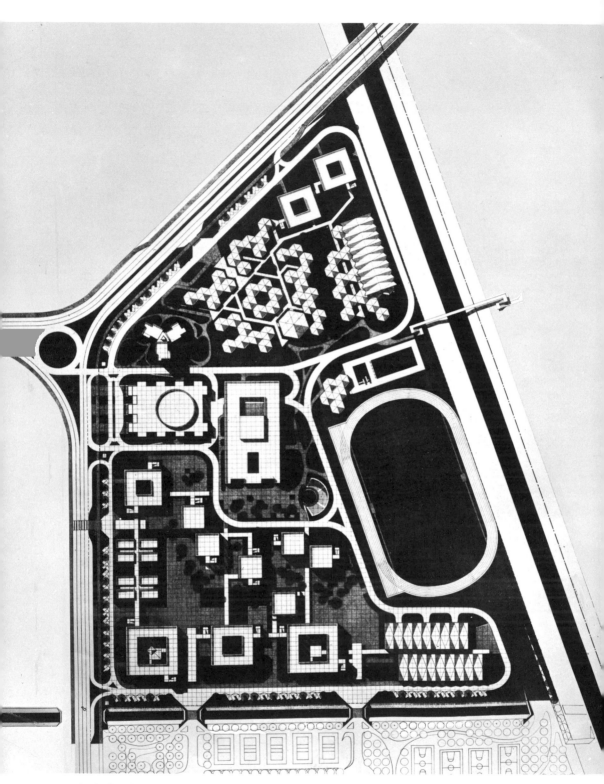

31. *José Ravelomanantsoa and Jean Rabemanantsoa: School Center, Anosy, the Malagasy Republic, plan.*

Two young Frenchmen sought to break new ground with their design for a parliament in Conakry, Guinea. Michel Andrault and Pierre Parat designed the building within the framework of the Beaux-Arts tradition but sought new, expressive forms of African origin. They planned a low, square complex with a slightly-raised, central roof-section lighting the partly open, partly closed interiors (*Fig. 32*). Although there are some details of the project which tend toward the picturesque—the roof structures and the battlements of the façade—it is one of the few designs by European architects which aims at something African. Regrettably the project has not been built.

In contrast to Andrault and Parat's design for Conakry are the formal cliches, monumental megalomania, and overloaded decoration which characterize the residences of many heads of state. There are no essential differences between the palace of the emperor in Addis Ababa, the seat of the president of Upper Volta in Wagadugu, the castle-like residence of the Tunisian president in Skanés, and the renovated Christianborg Castle near Accra for Ghana's chief of state.

As in Europe, the power of the state is reflected, above all, in the palaces of justice which house the apparatus of judicial administration. In Abidjan on the Ivory Coast, another building of the French colonial era has been taken over by a new government. Here, the

32. *Michel Andrault and Pierre Parat: Parliamentary buildings, Conakry, Guinea, model.*

French architects Badani and Roux-Dorlut had at least tried to find forms suited to the climate—within the Beaux-Arts vocabulary, of course—evidenced by the use of pierced walls.

The Moroccan architect Jean-François Zevaco continued to work within the French academic tradition, though in a progressive way, in the law courts at Ben Ahmed, Morocco (*Fig. 33*). For this building, which symbolizes the power of the law, he developed convincing, even tasteful and elegant forms; those with narrow, deep windows serve both for lighting and shading, and meet the conditions of the local climate. In his court buildings in Mohammedia (1962–1963) (*Figs. 34–36*) and Beni Mellal (*Fig. 37*), the treatment is developed with greater independence. Elie Azagury, also a Moroccan, deals with this problem in his Palace of Justice in Agadir. The free, loose treatment of the concrete seems further away from the French tradition, though still unmistakably based on it. The High Court in Kumasi, Ghana, like the State House in Kaduna, falls entirely within the British tradition. It was designed by the architects Nickson and Borys who also built the Central Magistrates Courts in Accra.

33. *Jean-François Zevaco: Law Courts, Ben Ahmed, Morocco.*

34. *Jean-François Zevaco: Palace of Justice, Mohammedia, Morocco, 1962–1963.*

35. *Jean-François Zevaco: Palace of Justice, Mohammedia.*

36. *Jean-François Zevaco: Palace of Justice, Mohammedia.*

37. *Jean-François Zevaco: Regional Tribunal, Beni-Mellal, Morocco, 1964.*

Appropriately designed city halls exist in only a few African states. Henri Chomette found a convincing vocabulary for the City Hall of Abidjan (*Fig. 38*). Though Chomette's forms are African only in their outward appearance, this is one of the few complexes in which a native community found architectural expression. The City Hall of Agadir by Arsène-Henry and Honnegger, built before 1960, was but one of the few buildings to survive the earthquake of that year. It now serves as the Ministry of the Interior. The Civic Center in Rabat, by Elie Azagury, represents a new departure both in conception and execution: functions of city administration are combined with cultural facilities. The core of this complex is a multipurpose hall for four hundred people around which administrative offices, a police station, a post office, and a café are grouped (*Figs. 39–42*).

The various embassy buildings, which have become necessary in the new capitals, are merely the architectural forms of foreign countries—often enriched with folkloric details—transplanted to Africa.

38. *Henri Chomette: City Hall, Abidjan, Ivory Coast, plan.*

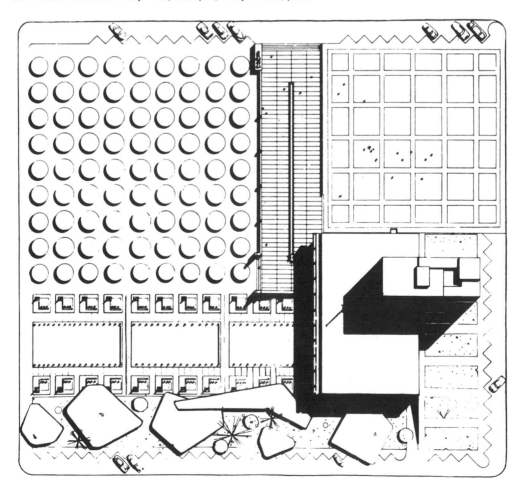

39. *Elie Azagury: Civic Center, Rabat, Morocco, view of main entrance, 1967.*

40. *Elie Azagury: Civic Center, Rabat, Morocco, view of the post office, 1967.*

41. *Elie Azagury: Civic Center, Rabat, Morocco, view of pilotis (pillars) and administrative offices, 1967.*

There are few differences between the German Embassy in Pretoria, South Africa, by Klaus Schwedhelm; the French Embassy in Kotonou, Dahomey, by Henri Chomette; the French Embassy in Lagos, Nigeria, by Ducharme, Martin, and Romig; or the American Embassy in Accra, Ghana, by Harry Weese—the most convincing of all.

Commercial

During the past century, office buildings—usually branches of European and American firms—have been built in cities like Johannesburg, Capetown, Cairo, Algiers, Casablanca, Lagos, Salisbury, and Dar-es-Salaam. They display the architectural concepts developed since the last quarter of the nineteenth century, and can be judged by the same standards as those in New York, London, Calcutta, or Buenos Aires. They employ the most efficient and economical layout of interior space as well as an impressive (and prestigious) façade.

In his African Life Center in Capetown, Monty Sack combined a horizontal public wing with a huge glass tower, opening up the high-rise architecture of the city after the model of New York City's Lever House. In Dar-es-Salaam, C. A. Bransgrove designed a dramatic-looking office building on a corner site which also consists of a tower and horizontal, curved units. The ground floor is largely given over to shops. In Ndola, Zambia, the architects Gluckman, De Beer, and Peters built Caravelle House, which combines shops and offices in four stories. In Paare, South Africa, the architects Uytenbogaert and Pelser built a shopping center which brings the city space into the building by interior passageways.

In West Africa, Godwin and Hopwood designed Hanbury House, on Tinubu Square in Lagos. The interior temperature of the building is regulated by the region's typical, and in this case movable, sun-shades. Two other office buildings by this team were built for the Northern Nigeria Newspapers and the Philips Company in Kaduna, northern Nigeria. Kenneth Scott's Bedford House in Accra, Ghana, contains automobile showrooms on the ground floor and offices above. The designs by Fry, Drake, Drew, and Lasdun for office buildings and banks in Accra and Ibadan owe their characteristic shape, articulated by sunshades, to the long experience of this British firm in West Africa.

The young Nigerian Ekwueme designed office buildings in several parts of Lagos for firms like Niger-Pools in Ijora Lagos, the West Africa Airways Corporation in Ikeja Lagos (*Fig. 44*), and the Nigeria Petroleum Refinery in Alesa Eleme, near Port Harcourt. These massive, somewhat lifeless structures do not yet measure up to international standards of quality. Considerably more interesting is the Kenya Federation of Labor Headquarters in Nairobi, commissioned by Tom Mboya (*Fig. 45*). The various and contrasting materials match the new will with a new style. Architect H. Richard Hughes kept the

42. *Elie Azagury: Civic Center, Rabat, Morocco, view of the west façade and post office, 1967.*

43. *Jean-François Zevaco: Post office, Agadir, Morocco, 1966.*

44. *A. Ifeanyi Ekwueme: West Africa Airways Corporation, Ikeja-Lagos, Nigeria.*

45. *H. Richard Hughes: Kenya Federation of Labor Headquarters, Nairobi, Kenya, council chamber viewed from the courtyard, 1960.*

irregular, slightly angular complex open on one side and closed on the other, and succeeded in meeting the needs of the program for this organization. Recent buildings by Hughes include the Development House (1968) and the Estelcoms House (1969–1970) in Nairobi.

Bank offices are becoming ever more necessary throughout the continent (the system of banking goes back for decades in South Africa) and have been built especially well in West Africa. In Accra, E. Maxwell Fry and Jane Drew designed a six-story glass tower, protected by sunshades, for the Cooperative Bank Offices. In another building, by Drake and Lasdun (of the firm Fry, Drew, Drake, and Lasdun), at Takoradi, and in the Cooperative Bank of Western Nigeria in Ibadan, the architects made even greater use of the tropical sunshade systems and created imaginative architectural forms.

Henri Chomette's Society General Bank in Brazzaville, the Congo Republic, combines a large banking hall on the ground floor with offices in the four upper stories. The interior plan derives from the French tradition; the imaginative façade (*Fig. 46*), recalling Le Corbusier's work in concrete, is particularly impressive as is Jean-François Zevaco's National Bank for Economic Development (*Fig. 47*).

The communications industry also creates a need for structures which can accommodate their special requirements. Zevaco's design for a radio and television station in Agadir has a roof whose characteristic shape is the result of housing apparatus for lights (*Fig. 48*). H. Richard Hughes designed the television center for the Kenya

46. *Henri Chomette: Society General Bank, Brazzaville, the Congo Republic.*

47. Jean-François Zevaco: National Bank for Economic Development, Rabat, Morocco, 1965.

48. Jean-François Zevaco: Radio and Television Station, Agadir, Morocco.

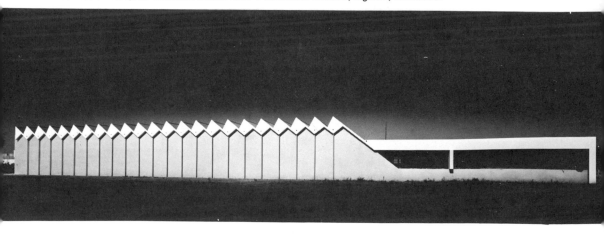

Broadcasting Corporation in Nairobi (1967) and the transmitting station for the Voice of Kenya in Ngong (1967). Oluwole Olumuyiwa built Crusaders' House in Lagos (*Fig. 49*).

A garage and auto-repair shop at Broken Hill, Zambia, by Julian Elliott, is noteworthy for its projecting (and shading) roof, which rests on slender supports and gives the glass-faced building its shape. The architects Berlowitz, Furmanowsky, and Kagan arrived at a similar solution in their big garage and auto-repair shop for Modern Motors, Ltd., in Bulawayo, Rhodesia, in which showrooms and workshops are arranged in two stories. In contrast to these buildings, which house multiple functions under one roof, Peer Abben designed the offices and workshops of the Cooper Motor Corporation Ltd., in Nairobi, as a loosely related complex of units, each having a different height.

49. *Oluwole Olumuyiwa: Crusaders' House, Lagos, Nigeria, detail of window panels at rear façade.*

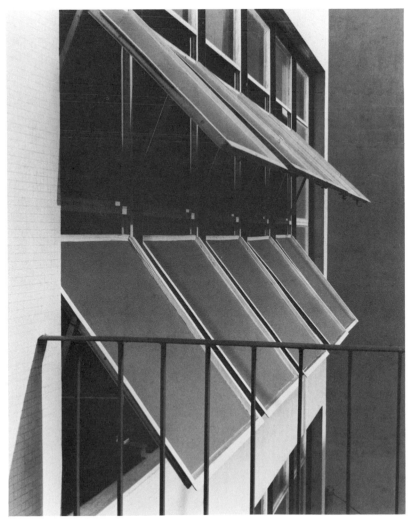

The earliest factories on the continent were constructed in South Africa, where the social organization and climate are most comparable to that of Europe and America. Berlowitz, Furmanowsky, and Kagan designed a long building for the Rhodesia Packing Factory in Bulawayo; two dynamically shaped wings are connected by narrow right-angled units to the similar, somewhat elevated, principal structure.

Apart from the European traditions of the Republic of South Africa, and (formerly French) North Africa, innovations in this important field have not yet been achieved. In North Africa, Auguste Perret had already designed docks in Casablanca and other Algerian cities like Saïda, Tiaret, and Sidi-bel-Abbes by the time of the First World War (1915), employing his pioneering shell construction. Factories receive little attention in black Africa because of the totally different conception of work; these countries are primarily agricultural, and the climate does not favor factory work.

Social and Cultural

The creation of institutions and buildings for social and cultural gatherings is well suited to the sociable, community-minded character of the African. In the past, the out-of-doors provided ample opportunity for congregation, keeping architectural needs to a minimum. Since the contact with European culture, and the flow of people into urban centers, social and cultural activities have increasingly moved indoors and must be housed.

In recent years, kindergartens have been built, such as the example by Amancio d'Alpoim Guedes in Lourenço Marques, intended for Portuguese children. Guedes, like Aldo van Eyck in his Children's House in Amsterdam, knows how to create spaces for children. The arrangement of smaller and larger spaces in the interior matches the effective exterior composition of pyramidal roofs and rectangular shapes. This happy solution cannot hide the fact that the kindergarten is an importation of a European custom and building genre. Guedes comes from the Portuguese tradition; the Tunisian architect Olivier-Clement Cacoub from the French. Cacoub modified this tradition in his Children's Center at Kassar Said, Tunisia (*Fig. 50*).

The area of social clubs has barely been developed in Africa. In Japan, for example, there are various clubs for sports, recreation, or cultural pursuits—designed for large-scale events—which are among the most successful expressions of the new style of Japanese architecture. In Africa, however, where everything is designed for education, there are relatively few cultural centers. Ernst May was able to create a pioneering center in Moshi, Tanzania, in which he combined a large auditorium, offices, shops, a hotel, and a restaurant (*Fig. 51*). In this case, the client was particularly important: the native African coffee planters commissioned the building to express the new com-

50. *Olivier-Clement Cacoub: Children's Center, Kassar Said, Tunisia.*

51. *Ernst May: Cultural Center, Moshi, Tanzania.*

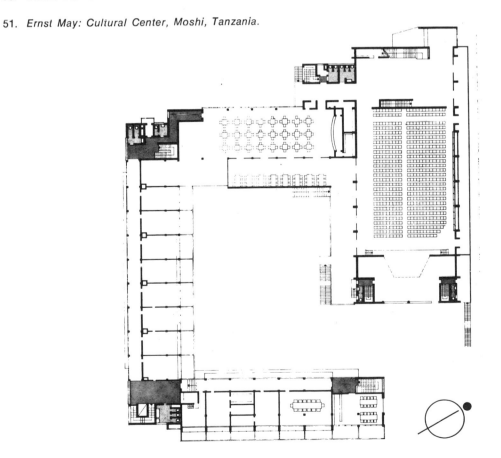

munity spirit. The British architects Peatfield and Bodgener arrived at an entirely different solution in their cultural center in Kampala, Uganda, in the European tradition, built by Europeans in Africa for Europeans; several activities are grouped around a central theatre.

The three most fascinating projects for cultural centers are still on the drawing board: 1) a center in Leopoldville in the Republic of the Congo, by Takamasa Yoshizaka, whose design won first prize in an international competition; 2) the Cité des Arts for Senegal, proposed by Marcello d'Olivo; and 3) a community center in Lagos by Oluwole Olumuyiwa.

Yoshizaka's plan calls for an essentially closed complex with two auditoriums and, in between, an outdoor museum and a museum with a study center (*Fig. 52*). By an imaginative linking of dynamic, curved forms—not only in the auditoriums but also in the long, partly cavelike rooms of the study center—Yoshizaka developed an architecture appropriate for Africa, one which could have considerable influence on the evolution of architecture throughout the continent.

D'Olivo groups the various cultural buildings (library, dancing school, museum, and so on) in an open three-quarter circle punctuated with forms characterized by triangles in elevation and layout. This design is also capable of giving new impetus to African architecture (*Fig. 53*).

The cultural center planned for Lagos by Olumuyiwa is conceived as a combined technical institute, teachers' college, and community center (*Fig. 54*). At the heart of the complex—which recalls the manner of the Dutch team of Van den Broek and Bakema—stands an elevated entrance area with offices, assembly hall, two-story foyer, and music rooms; it leads to an area with workshops around a rectangular court. The gymnasium (with a glass barrel-vault) and a lower-level area with kitchen and dining rooms are set off.

The large parking lot at the entrance is separated by a wall from the garden next to the gymnasium; the upper platform of the gymnasium is reached by a ramp. Olumuyiwa planned an outdoor theatre between the entrance and dining areas, and a sculpture garden to supplement interior exhibition space. His well-conceived and appropriate design still betrays the influences absorbed during his training in Britain, the Netherlands, and Switzerland.

There are relatively few theatres in Africa, apart from the National Theatre in Kampala, Uganda, by Peatfield and Bodgener, and the Western-style theatres in the Republic of South Africa. Drama and dance are popular in a very different way from our own, and nature offers enough usable open space to make a roof unnecessary in most cases.

Among the few African theatres, the following deserve mention: the Study Theatre in Accra, by Gerlach and Gillies-Reyburn; the theatre in Kikuyu by H. Richard Hughes, which also doubles as an

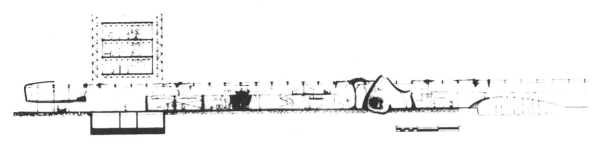

52. *Takamasa Yoshizaka: Cultural Center, Leopoldville, the Congo Republic, project.*

53. *Marcello d'Olivo: Cité des Arts, Senegal, project.*

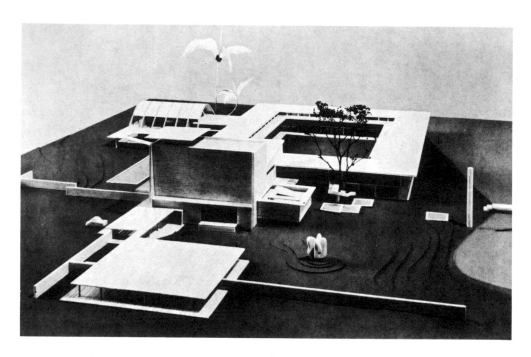

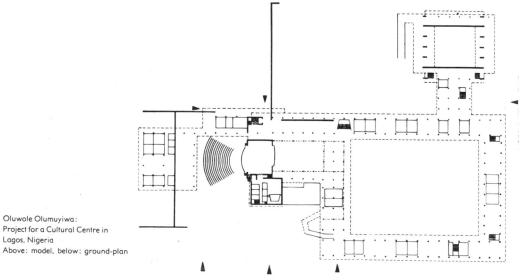

Oluwole Olumuyiwa:
Project for a Cultural Centre in
Lagos, Nigeria
Above: model, below: ground-plan

54. *Oluwole Olumuyiwa: Cultural Center, Lagos, project.*

assembly hall for the Alliance High School; and the theatre project for Dakar, developed by the sculptor André Bloc with architect Claude Parent, engineer René Sarger, and theatre expert Jacques Polieri. The latter building was planned as an organically-rounded, closed form in the style of Bloc's sculpture.

There are also few museums, aside from those in South Africa or Egypt, which again show the overwhelming dominance of Western styles. A significant exception is the National Museum in Accra, by the architects Drake and Lasdun. Here a low, rectangular base is surmounted by a gently vaulted dome.

Libraries play a fundamental role in the independent nations. They have usually been constructed as part of other institutions, such as colleges, throughout the continent and are of substantial quality. Among the college libraries, the University Library in Ibadan, by Fry, Drew, Drake, and Lasdun, and the University Library in Kampala, by Norman and Dawbarn, deserve mention. The library has also been placed in the center of the campus in other recent college complexes; other examples are the clearly articulated library in Port Harcourt, by James Cubitt, which is reached by a fiat, wide entrance ramp. Others are the Eastern Region Library in Koforidua, Ghana, by Kenneth Scott, lighted by a band of glass below the projecting roof; and the library for the British Council in Kadura, by Goodwin and Hopwood. The firm of Nickson and Borys has also built libraries: the Central Library in Accra, which includes a children's department with a sculptured entrance wall, and the Padmore Memorial Library in Accra, a small building, partly on supports, with a rounded front wall. Julian Elliott proposed a public library for Ndola, Zambia, having cubelike units radiating from a square, central unit with square roof structures.

All these buildings and projects are by British architects. Though located in widely different parts of the continent, each building displays a design based upon practical needs, a characteristic of the works of British architects in Africa. The Teachers' Reference Library in Lagos by Oluwole Olumuyiwa is the first effort by a young African architect in Nigeria (*Fig. 55*).

Religious

Church buildings are problematic because of the variety of coexisting and competing religions. Christian, that is, missionary, churches exist, of course, throughout the continent, and are naturally identified with colonialism. Expressions of a new approach to Christianity have seldom been effective.

An example of church architecture in West Africa is the University Chapel in Ibadan by George G. Pace; the clearly vaulted nave and a free-standing stone bell tower recall early Christian buildings. The tendency toward fortress-like, elementary forms is given stronger bent in Pace's project for a cathedral in Ibadan.

In East Africa, H. Richard Hughes built various churches for the Kikuyus. In the Krapf-Rebman Memorial Church in Kilifi, Kenya, he contrasted concrete and brick, and stone and glass in a convincing manner. The sloped building, with a squat, rectangular tower open at the top, expressed a new concept in a Christian church demanded by the Kikuyus (*Figs. 56–57*).

The Swiss Justus Dahinden tried to create prototypes for Catholic churches which are determined by basic African forms. He also attempted to establish a relationship between Christianity and an ancient African cult centered on dancing. Whether such renewal meets the real demands of African society is questionable. Dahinden built, for instance, pilgrimage churches in Uganda and always attempted to find a suitably designed church for the African. He derived

55. *Oluwole Olumuyiwa: Teachers' Reference Library, Lagos.*

56. *H. Richard Hughes: Krapf-Rebman Memorial Church, Kilifi, Kenya, view from north.*

57. *H. Richard Hughes: Krapf-Rebman Memorial Church, Kilifi, Kenya, ground plan.*

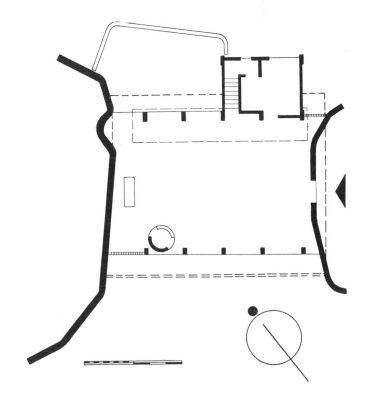

58. *Godwin and Hopwood: Northern Police College, mosque, Kaduna, Nigeria, 1963.*

59. *Architects' Co-Partnership: Bristol Hotel, Lagos, 1692.*

the layout of his village church in Toussiana, Volta, from the shape of the African dance mask; he placed a low, exposed area visible from all sides, corresponding to the ancient African dance ground, in front of the altar, the center of the sacrificial service. E. Ladner built a village church with dance ground in Koumi, Upper Volta, and P. Brunner designed a bush church, made out of plant materials like a hut.

Little can be said about the architecture of the mosque, which is far more important for Africa. Mosques are rarely included in larger complexes, as at the Northern Police College in Kaduna, by Godwin and Hopwood (*Fig. 58*). The ceremonial function of Islam in the cities and suburbs takes place mostly in emergency buildings; they are needed and put up in great numbers without aesthetic or constructive considerations.

The situation of religious architecture in Africa makes clear that the importation of clichés or superficially "modern" forms will not work. This is one area where architects must bypass the well-worn paths in order to arrive at designs which are based upon reality and not on the wishful thinking of established organizations.

Hotels and Restaurants

The building of hotels and restaurants plays an important part in most regions in view of the steadily growing tourist trade. Many hotels in Africa meet the international standards; often belonging to European or American corporations, these hotels take over their architectural form from the West. For example, Welton Beckett's Cairo Hilton is stylistically in the American vein. The Hôtel de France in Conakry, by Guy Lagneau, belongs to a French hotel chain and reflects this.

Hotels have also been built in connection with newly-planned industries. For example, Guy Lagneau's hotel with restaurant attached was one of numerous commissions in the Cité Alucam at Édea, Cameroon. The simple, economical building on supports is appropriate. The hotels by Henri Chomette are similar. In Cocody near Abidjan, Chomette built a hotel within a newly-opened lake area; it consists of a four-story main building with a round umbrella-roofed restaurant overlooking the lake shore, and several buildings on ground which slopes down toward the lake.

The enlarged Avenida Hotel in Accra by Kenneth Scott displays a concept of simple, economical, and clear forms. The British firm Architects' Co-Partnership built two hotels in Lagos: one, a large building on a marina dates from the fifties, and the other, the Bristol, standing in the center of the Nigerian capital, was completed in 1962 (*Fig. 59*). Other possibilities in this field were realized by the architects Berlowitz, Furmanovsky, and Kagan in their small, clearly structured drive-in restaurant in Buluwayo, Rhodesia, and by Castelneau and Tastemain in their City University Restaurant in Rabat (1963).

Entirely new concepts were carried out in the development of vacation villages in North and East Africa, which combine swimming and sports facilities, in addition to a hotel, restaurant, and other tourits attractions. In 1966, H. Richard Hughes built the Watamu Beach Hotel near Malindi in deliberately "historic" style directly on the coast (*Figs. 60, 117*). Castelneau and Tastemain designed the Centre Balnéaire in Skhirat, Morocco, which includes hotel, restaurant, bar, and baths. Olivier-Clement Cacoub built a vacation village at Skanés, Tunisia, where the streets and squares are integrated in the plan (*Figs. 61–62*). Eli Azagury built the vacation village Cabo Negro on the Mediterranean coast of Morocco: here hotels, restaurants, bathing, and sports facilities form an integrated ensemble of convincing quality (*Figs. 63–64*).

Hospitals

Hospitals in Africa have a tradition, particularly in Morocco and South Africa, which is of course un-African. The large building by the Frenchmen Delaporte, Bonnemaison and Robert in Rabat is an example. Other hospitals in Morocco were built by Bousquet in Marrakech and by Chemineau and Pocioli in Quezzane. Castelneau and Tastemain designed the dispensary in Kenitra. The Moroccan Jean-François Zevaco created the small Hopital Complementaire in Ben Slimane; it is a longitudinal stone building with projecting concrete forms (*Fig. 65*). The central hospital in Nouakchott in Upper Volta is

60. *H. Richard Hughes: Watamu Beach Hotel, near Malindi, Kenya, main building with water tank and cottages on cliff.*

61. *Olivier-Clement Cacoub: Tourist Center, Skanés, Tunisia, 1966.*

62. *Olivier-Clement Cacoub: Tourist Center, Skanés, Tunisia, 1966.*

63. *Elie Azagury: Tourist Center, Cabo Negro, Morocco, 1968.*

64. *Elie Azagury: Hotel "Petit Merou," Cabo Negro, Morocco, 1968.*

by the architects Jean Louis Véret, Bérard Thurnauer, Jean Renaudie and Pierre Riboulet.

In West Africa, the hospital in Kurle Bu, near Accra in Ghana, by William F. Vetter and Kenneth Scott, deserves special mention. The multi-wing complex, articulated by sunshades and roof structures, contains 860 beds. Pediatrics, surgery, women's clinic and other special facilities, and the nearby residences for doctors and nurses, are parts of the institution.

The hundred-bed hospital for the Nigerian Railway Corporation in Ebutametta, near Lagos, by Ekwueme, was the first hospital by an African architect. The multi-wing plan appears repetitive but Ekwueme was able to do justice to this commission which required special expertise (*Fig. 66*).

Attempts to erect hospitals with very simple, traditional building materials, are not always successful. For example, a hospital in Northern Nigeria was built of clay, which does not meet the special requirements of this task.

65. *Jean-François Zevaco: Hospital, Ben-Slimane, Morocco.*

Stadiums

Sports stadiums in Africa have been designed almost exclusively by Europeans. At Kumasi, Ghana, Kenneth Scott created a powerful shape for the covered, concrete grandstand, thereby marking the direction of the access ramps. The roof tilts slightly back and is far forward from a center row of columns. Scott exploits the technical possibilities of the material by employing a principle first used in 1935 by Eduardo Torroja at the racecourse, La Zarzuela, near Madrid. J. E. K. Harrison's steel forms for the press box and scoreboard at the large Liberty stadium in Ibadan, have a somewhat stiffer effect, but his solution is nevertheless appropriate. The Uganda Sports Union Headquarters at Kampala, Uganda, by Peatfield and Bodgener, is comparable to the Kumasi Stadium. Here, too, the hovering effect of the roof over the grandstand is worth noting. All three of these structures have been built under relatively unsophisticated circumstances and usually with limited financing. While this is characteristic of building in Africa at the present time, such conditions enforce solutions and do not necessarily have a negative effect.

66. *A. Ifeanyi Ekwueme: Hospital for Nigerian Railway Corporation, Ebute Metta, Lagos, Nigeria.*

If the project for a big stadium in Kampala, Uganda, by the Swedes Fritz Jaenicke and Sten Samuelson, had been carried out, it would have brought their special experience to African soil. In their scheme, the grandstand roof is integrated with one side of the oval, high, ramplike frame on supports, giving the project a dynamic spirit. The use of concrete informs the structures which Olivier-Clement Cacoub built for the Olympic Games complex in Tunis. The roof of the Sports Palace, resting on strong concrete supports, shelters the glass-walled substructure.

Market Halls

The market has traditionally been a vital institution for the African—especially the Central African. In many tribes everyone is both a buyer and a seller; everyone participates in the trade of goods. In many parts of the continent, a simple roof is sufficient to shade fruits, vegetables, and other perishable goods from the sun. The market in Abidjan, on the Ivory Coast, is a typical example for which Henri Chomette found a simple, practical, economical, and effective solution (*Fig. 67*).

67. *Henri Chomette: Market, Abidjan, Ivory Coast.*

Marcel Lods designed the market in Wagadugu, south of the Sahara. The goal was to achieve the largest possible shady and well-aired space. This huge, projecting structure on supports is covered in the center by a hanging roof (*Fig. 68*).

In Sidi-bel-Abbes, Algeria, Marcel Mauri built a dome-shaped roof with pointlike windows which admit light into the cool, shady interior (*Fig. 69*). The Moroccan architects Tastemain and Castelneau designed the municipal market hall in Taza. In contrast to the usual domed buildings, the architects have created a system of passages meeting at right angles; with a stand of old trees nearby they form a shady, picturesque spot in the center of town. Reinforced concrete is successfully combined here with stone and other traditional materials.

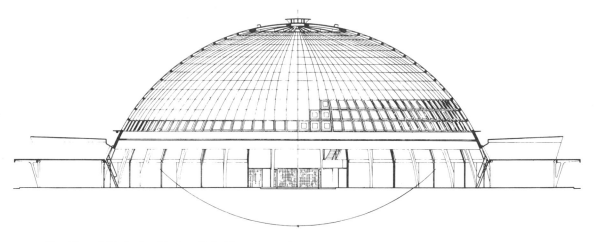

68. *Marcel M. Lods: Market Hall, Wagadugu, Chad, project.*

69. *Marcel Mauri: Market Hall, Sidi-bel-Abbes, Algeria.*

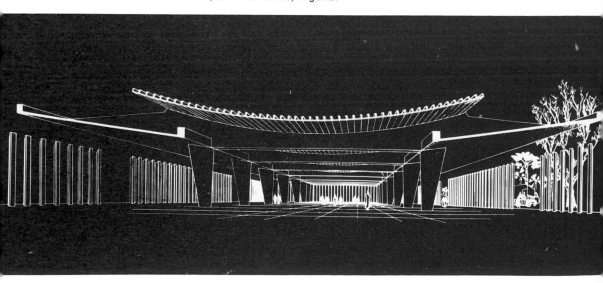

Exhibitions

More than any other type of building, the international or regional trade-fair pavilion shows the influence foreign architects have on the African architectural scene. In most cases, these pavilions are planned and built by architects from the exhibiting nations. The German pavilion at the Nairobi agricultural exhibition of 1961, for example, was designed by Theodor Raschkow who attempted to find open forms sympathetic to the setting and created a building with a wavy roof, and a pool which he integrated with the complex. The German pavilion at the industrial exhibition in Khartoum in 1961, by Georg Lippsmeyer and F. Reiser, was constructed of prefabricated elements which were mantled and dismantled on the site, thus becoming an exhibit attraction.

In his pavilion for the City of Casablanca at the 1960 international trade fair in Casablanca, Jean-François Zevaco tried to make the material—concrete—an exhibit. The shape of a pyramid resting on its apex exemplified the dramatic and constructive potentials of concrete (*Fig. 70*). This formal, even formalistic, kind of architecture is clearly indebted to the Brazilian architect Oscar Niemeyer.

A great many of the other trade fairs held throughout Africa have produced architecture of diverse origins; however, they displayed no innovations, or forms of African character.

70. *Jean-François Zevaco and E. J. Duhon: Pavilion of the city of Casablanca, International Fair of Casablanca, 1960.*

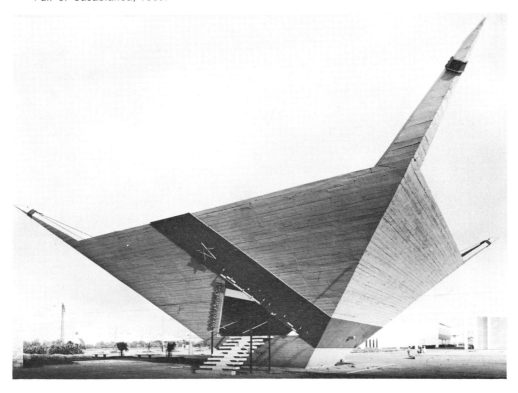

Transportation

Though modern transportation plays an important part in Africa, few appropriate solutions had resulted up to 1968. Railroad stations are no longer very important in Africa; the railroad is already obsolete. On the other hand, roads, garages, repair shops, and gas stations for the constantly growing automobile traffic have not yet produced designs which approach Western standards; there are some exceptions in Central and Southern Africa, especially the structures by Julian Elliott.

Air transportation, which is so crucial to Africa, has not yet found convincing architectural expression, though airport buildings have been erected in most of the states. Exceptions are airport buildings in Leopoldville by Claude Laurens, in Freetown by Nickson and Borys, and in Accra by Norman and Dawbarn. Although the continent with its vast, partly inaccessible, area is especially dependent on air transportation, the airports of Africa do not match the revolutionary élan of contemporary designs which have been developed in America and in some European countries.

More critical are the deficiencies in road building and planning, city planning, and bridge construction. Only the first and most urgent tasks have been started, and they have been completed only in a few places. Even where city plans exist or have been executed—for example, the Place Lapalud and related bridge construction by French architects in Abidjan on the Ivory Coast—the conceptions are so strongly within the European tradition that they remain alien elements in Africa. Even the city and traffic plans carried out in Casablanca reflect much past and obsolete thinking; they do not begin to express the African concept of dynamic living. The beginnings of fitting solutions appear in the reconstruction of the Moroccan city of Agadir which was destroyed by an earthquake in 1960.

Housing

Single-Family Houses

It is difficult to present a coherent picture of the single-family house in Africa, or even to find the indigenous element among the various groups. The need for this type of building, in the European or American sense, has never existed there. The African usually lived in a large community, and his farmlike settlements corresponded to his essentially polygamous way of life. His houses, not intended for one family in the narrow sense, consisted of groupings of closed and open rooms; they formed a whole in which both privacy and communication were possible. The single-family house, of which there are a number of successful examples in Africa, is of non-African origin and was mostly built for Europeans.

In the Republic of South Africa the single-family house is in the

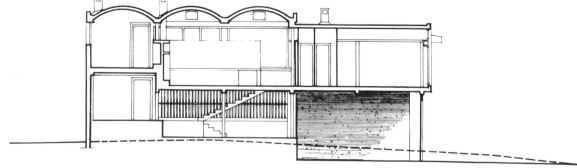

71. *P. A. Emery and L. Miquel: House, Alger, Algeria.*

Dutch, British, or American tradition; in Algeria it is in the French tradition, as expressed in buildings by Emery and Miquel (*Fig. 71*); in West Africa it is in the British tradition. British forms of tropical architecture include well-studied and valid solutions: the home by E. Maxwell Fry and Jane Drew in Lagos (*Fig. 72*); houses by the firm of Godwin and Hopwood; the Gottschalk house in Kano (*Fig. 73*); the Easmon House in Accra, by Kenneth Scott, or his steel-framed houses in Tesano near Accra. In this context belong various houses for professors at the University of Kumasi, Ghana, by James Cubitt, or the East African buildings by Peer Abben, similar to houses in Nairobi or Muthaiga, which are planned for standardization (*Fig. 74*).

Ernst May had earlier designed standardized houses for a society which urgently needs new forms of building and housing, but such designs remain exceptions. Even young African architects from West and North Africa follow the social and architectural conceptions of the European single-family house. They build homes for the small family, a social unit of Western civilization. For the most part what distinctive residential architecture there is in Africa is the work of foreigners: Arthur Swift in Liberia, Anthony Almeida in Dar-es-Salaam, Henri Chomette in Addis Ababa, Nickson and Borys in Lagos, Berlowitz and Furmanovsky in Bulawayo, Becker and Voigt in Lagos, Julian Elliott in Ndola and Itawa, and Amancio d'Alpoim Guedes in Lourenço Marques, Mozambique.

In his house in Ndola, Julian Elliott intended a specifically African solution with simple materials and forms adapted to the vegetation, evident already in his earlier buildings (*Figs. 75–76*). The huge roof-shell, supported only in the center, of the house in Itawa is developed out of the regional situation though the layout recalls neo-plastic principles of design (*Fig. 77*).

Kenneth Scott built a home, away from his architectural office in the city, outside Accra (*Fig. 78*). The living room, on the second floor, is marked by a large, open balcony, its supports, and sunshades. The architect H. Richard Hughes has combined his home and studio in Nairobi; his architectural office is below the living quarters. This low-cost house, built from 1956 to 1958, is a typical regional solution for a European in Africa. The Moroccan Elie Azagury also combined home and architectural office in Casablanca (*Figs. 79–81*), but they are separated by a garden. The office is reached from another street. The forms, derived from the French tradition, show typical African features in a way that will never be possible for transplanted Europeans. Azagury is an African whose European training is modified by his native traditions, thus enabling him to achieve an individual expression.

72. *E. Maxwell Fry, Jane Drew, Lindsay Drake, and Denys Lasdun: House, Lagos, Nigeria.*

73. *Architects' Co-Partnership: House, Kano, Nigeria.*

74. *Peer Abben: House, Nairobi (project).*

75. *Julian Elliott: House, Northrise, Zambia.*

76. *Julian Elliott: House, Ndola, Zambia, 1966.*

77. *Julian Elliott: House, Itawa, Zambia.*

78. *Kenneth Scott: House of the architect, Accra, Ghana.*

79. *Elie Azagury: House of the architect, Casablanca, Morocco.*

80. *Elie Azagury: Office of the architect, Casablanca, Morocco.*

81. *Elie Azagury: House, Casablanca, Morocco.*

82. *Amancio d'Alpoim Guedes: Smiling Lion Apartments, Lourenço Marques, Mozambique.*

83. *Amancio d'Alpoim Guedes: Miguel Bombard Terrace, Lourenço Marques, Mozambique.*

Multiple Dwellings and Housing Developments

Far more important than the single-family home for African architecture, is the grouping of houses, or rather the grouping of closed and open rooms into an organic whole. High-rise apartment houses and housing developments have existed in Johannesburg and North Africa for decades. The high-rise apartment houses built by Harold H. Le Roith in 1952 could stand in a London suburb. This also applies to similar buildings by S. A. Abramovitch and David Pinshow, and by numerous other architects in Johannesburg, Cape-town, Casablanca, Cairo, Algiers, Oran, Nairobi, and many other African cities. An example is the Cosmos Apartments in Bulawayo, Rhodesia, by the architects Berlowitz, Furmanovsky, and Kagan with the collaboration of the engineer Ove Arup. They created a realistic and practical combination of business architecture and luxury apartments.

With his proposal for 378 apartments in the center of Nairobi, Peer Abben sought a new order of high-rise buildings in the city's core. In Lourenço Marques, Amancio d'Alpoim Guedes built the Smiling Lion Apartments and Miguel Bombard Terrace *(Figs. 82–83)*. Yona Friedman, in collaboration with the engineer S. Ketof and the city planner R. Aujame, sought to apply urban super- and mega-structures with hanging compartments to the African situation (Abidjan, Niamey, Tunis; *Fig. 103*). Arthur Quarmby has designed emergency accommodations for Africans *(Fig. 84)*.

Africa does not require so much the transplanting of European designs with groups of preconceived cellular units as it does fitting solutions to problems which should be of specifically African character. It does not matter whether the author of such a project is English or African.

A few projects in this direction have already been realized. In the vicinity of Christiansborg Castle, the seat of Ghana's head of state near Accra, the young British architect D. A. Barrett, working in the Department of Public Construction (D.P.C.) in Accra, has developed a housing project conceived for Africans, namely the employees at Christiansborg Castle *(Figs. 85–88)*. The architect related a loosely grouped series of single-family houses in a way which is not merely additive but productive. The projecting and receding houses enclose a courtyard which corresponds to the open space of the traditional compound. In the precisely studied plan block A is related to blocks B and C at a right angle. The open, short side of the courtyard is closed by the communal laundry.

Each house has closed and open spaces. It contains a private inner courtyard and relatively small rooms in several stories which are reached by exterior and interior stairs. It is a varied, plastic, spatial ensemble, entirely contemporary, which meets both present demands

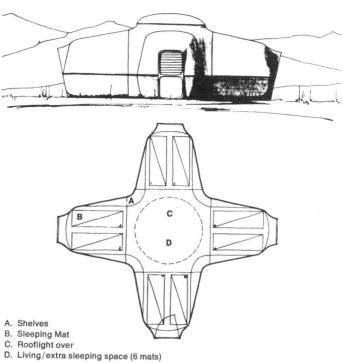

A. Shelves
B. Sleeping Mat
C. Rooflight over
D. Living/extra sleeping space (6 mats)

84. *Arthur Quarmby: Prefabricated houses for Africa, project.*

85. *D. A. Barrett and D.P.C.: Housing near the Christiansborg Castle, Accra, Ghana, 1962.*

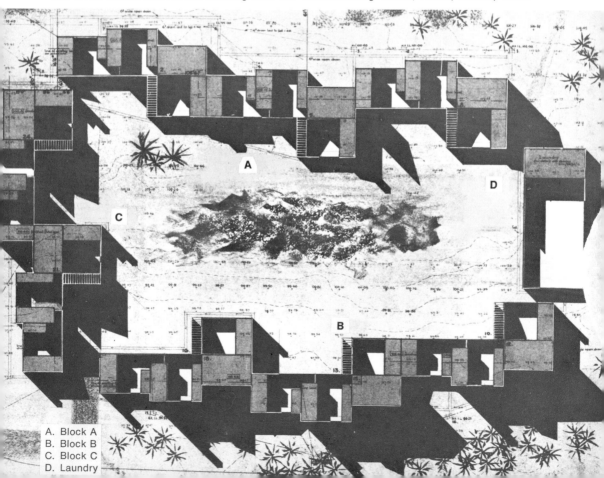

A. Block A
B. Block B
C. Block C
D. Laundry

86. *D. A. Barrett and D.P.C.: Housing near the Christiansborg Castle, Accra, Ghana, model, 1962.*

87. *D. A. Barrett and D.P.C.: Housing near the Christiansborg Castle, Accra, Ghana, 1962.*

and uses the constants of African traditions imaginatively. The settlement, in a small pine-grown valley, is a pioneering example for a new African architecture, though still at an experimental stage. It is significant because, unlike imports of alien forms, it accepts the polygamous community life of the African.

A second pioneering settlement was also created by an Englishman, Julian Elliott, in Katanga (*Figs. 89–90*). It grew out of the same principles as the West African project, but is intended for Europeans living in Africa. Here also, the relation of closed and open rooms to the whole design plays a part. In 1956 and 1957, Elliott in collaboration with Philippe Charbonnier, grouped six apartments around a square inner courtyard. Although these homes are intended for immigrant white families, the architect specifically followed African concepts. He formulated them in a letter, referring to the great ruins of Zimbabwe:

> We always return to this planning solution and the concept of "solid boxes in open boxes," which seems such a characteristic of buildings in Africa—the beehive villages in Ghana, Mapogga, in the Northern Transvaal and possibly the finest and most monumental of all, the Zimbabwe ruins of Southern Rhodesia, really an exceptional example of the defined and moulded roofless or external space.

88. *D. A. Barrett and D.P.C.: Housing near the Christiansborg Castle, Accra, Ghana.*

89. *Julian Elliott and Philippe Charbonnier: Housing, Elizabethville, Katanga, model of Group 1, 1956–1957.*

In Central and South Africa we are dealing with isolated projects; in North Africa, especially Algeria and Morocco, projects have already been realized on a large scale. Here, too, the need is for mass housing with attention to climate and traditional living habits. From these, new contemporary forms must be developed. In Algeria, the work of Roland Simounet is especially noteworthy; he has built single-family homes in El Biar and simple housing developments in Berard. His masterpiece is the terrace settlement in Djennan-el-Hassan, the so-called Cité de Recasement which recalls the original North African tradition, like the buildings of Medinine (*Figs. 91–92*). Long before 1960 Simounet developed architectural ideas and forms which have only been realized and elaborated very recently. At Djennan-el-Hassan he used the different levels of the hilly site as a meaningful point of departure for a new concept of settlement. He fits the homes into the landscape like cells in a honeycomb and achieves a close integration of housing and nature (*Fig. 93*). In the Malagasy Republic, the native architects José Ravelomanantsoa, Jean Ratamatanantsoa, and Jean Rabemanantsoa have achieved noteworthy results both in the construction of economical row houses at Tananarive, and in the development of a whole new living quarter at Ampefilolia (*Figs. 94–95*).

Mass housing had far larger effects upon the native population in cities like Casablanca, Oran, Algiers, or Saida, where it has been built on a large scale after the concepts of Georges Candilis and Shadrach Woods (*Fig. 96*), but partly after those of the Moroccan architects Zevaco (in Marrakesh) and Azagury (in Casablanca and Agadir). In Algeria, Candilis worked with M. J. Mauri and Dennis Pons, in Sidi-bel-Abbes, Oran, and elsewhere (*Fig. 97*). The principle of Georges Candilis' Habitat Musulman, designed as early as 1953, is the massing of simple and economical standardized apartments in five-story cellular row houses. Each apartment has a private balcony which can be used as an outdoor room. The arrangement of the elements in the required construction has led to solutions which are also esthetically convincing.

90. *Julian Elliott and Philippe Charbonnier: Housing, Elizabethville, Katanga, Group II, 1957.*

91. *Roland Simounet: Cité de Recasement, Djennan-el-Hassan, Algeria.*

92. *Roland Simounet: Cité de Recasement, Djennan-el-Hassan, Algeria.*

94. *José Ravelomanantsoa, Jean Rafamatanantsoa, and Jean Rabemanantsoa: Unité Résidentielle, Ampefilolia, Tananarive, the Malagasy Republic.*

95. *José Ravelomanantsoa, Jean Rafamatanantsoa, and Jean Rabemanantsoa: Unité Résidentielle, Ampefilolia, Tananarive, the Malagasy Republic.*

96. *Georges Candilis and Shadrach Woods: Apartments, Casablanca, Morocco.*

97. *M. J. Mauri, Georges Candilis, and Dennis Pons: Apartments, Oran, Algeria.*

Besides Candilis, the Swiss André Studer has worked on housing developments for Arabs in Casablanca; he was able to build them in 1954–1955. Studer also provides private outdoor rooms in the upper stories. He groups diagonal rows and multistory point buildings around a central marketplace (*Fig. 98*).

Besides the model mass housing for Africans in Casablanca by the Europeans Candilis and Studer, there are also a number of works by Moroccan architects. In Agadir, the architects Faraoui, de Mazières, and Ichter built model developments after the earthquake. Elie Azagury also arrived at new solutions in his developments in Casablanca and Rabat. In Rabat he grouped single-family houses so that the standardized spaces and solids produce a novel spatial ensemble. The articulation of windows and walls is derived from Europe, but the principle of the expandable development with court-yards and terraces is significant. Tradition has been revived here for a new North African architecture; it is quite evident in the roof gardens, balconies, sheltered shady spaces, and the closed building forms which protect the interior from outside view.

Azagury's development in Casablanca depends on the stacking of three stories which are carried out in the simplest and most eco-

98. *André Studer and Jean Hentsch: Apartments, Casablanca, Morocco, 1953–1954.*

nomical manner. Walls and somewhat formalistic panels alternate with windows and pierced walls for ventilating the open interior rooms (*Fig. 99*). It may seem paradoxical that new architectural expressions have been found for housing the large families of a polygamous society. The oriental way of life, characterized by the different status of women, has led native and foreign architects to convincing and exemplary solutions. They are also valid for other parts of the world.

99. *Elie Azagury: Office and apartment building, Casablanca, Morocco, 1968.*

CITY PLANNING

THE major urban problem in Africa, as elsewhere, is city planning—the reorganization and renewal of whole cities on new principles which accept the African reality. Beginnings exist in some regions. For example, in East Africa Ernst May designed a project for the redevelopment of some districts in Kampala (Kampala Extension Scheme). Le Corbusier had repeatedly worked on plans for North African cities. The architects Emery and Miquel developed the 1944 plan for the renewal of the city of Berrovaghia in Algeria which they carried out with Breuillot. The architects A. Daure and H. Beri with Roland Simounet created the design for the Cité La Montagne at Hussein-Dey, Algeria; they combined two thousand homes for low-income residents, five hundred rental apartments, and a thousand single-family homes.

In neighboring Tunisia, Olivier-Clement Cacoub developed the plan for the satellite city of Kabaria near Tunis and its Civic Center. Cacoub here arrived at a plan of residential sections with greenbelts around a business and cultural core. The German Max Guther and his collaborator Peter Petzold developed the new capital of Ethiopia, Bahar-Dar on Lake Tana, with a government center, ministries, imperial villa, and extensive residential sections toward the shores of the lake. The plan has since been carried out with changes by Bulgarian architects. Candilis, Josic, and Woods have prepared the plans for a new city on Lake Chad.

Various plans by Guy Lagneau, M. Weill and J. Dimitrijevic in West Africa are also noteworthy: for example, the Cité de Cansado in Mauretania, and Édea in Cameroon, in collaboration with the engineer René Sarger (*Figs. 100–101*). These cities in newly opened industrial regions, had to be created out of nothing, complete with stores, schools, restaurants, hotels, clubs, and all technical facilities. Most buildings in Édea date from the late fifties. The aluminum factory was built in 1957. Lagneau, Weill, and Dimitrijevic developed Porte Étienne on the frontier with the Spanish Sahara by the Cité de Cansado, a basically rectangular plan with business centers at the core and outer residential sections (*Fig. 100*).

The various projects by Yona Friedman and J. T. Pequet for the border regions of the Sahara and for large North African cities have not yet gone beyond the planning stage (*Figs. 102–103*). The continuation of old African traditions with the use of new materials may also

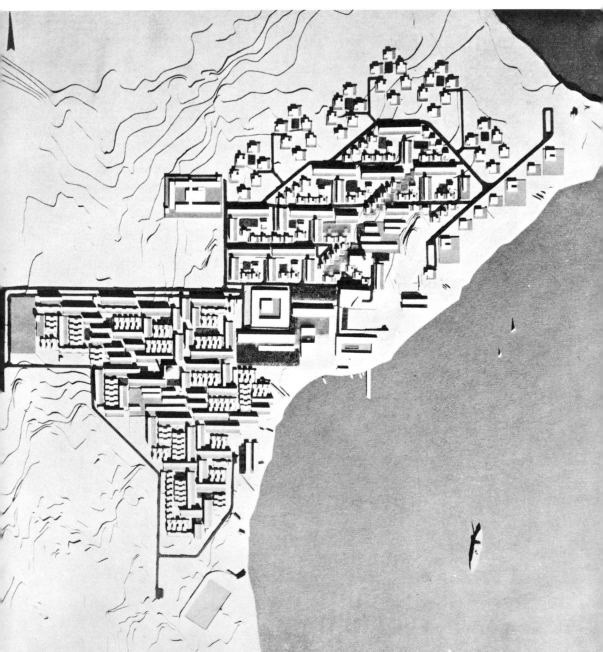

100. *Guy Lagneau, M. Weill, and J. Dimitrijevic: Cité de Cansado, Port Étienne, Mauretania.*

lead Yona Friedman to creative new thinking. David Olatunde Aradeon has prepared plans for the redevelopment of the city of Agbaja in southern Nigeria.

One of the most important achievements of African architecture is the rebuilding of Agadir, which was almost entirely destroyed by earthquake in 1960. It was carried out in large-scale collaboration by Moroccan architects working with new concepts. Pierre Mas, Mourad Ben Embarek, Claude Beurret, and Jean-Paul Ichter played an important part in working out the plans. Riou and Tastemain were responsible for laying out the city center, the important public buildings were designed by Elie Azagury, and the residential buildings were designed by Faraoui and de Mazierès (*Fig. 104*). Here, a new standard was successfully translated into reality.

101. *Guy Lagneau, M. Weill, and J. Dimitrijevic: Cité Alucam, Édea, Cameroon.*

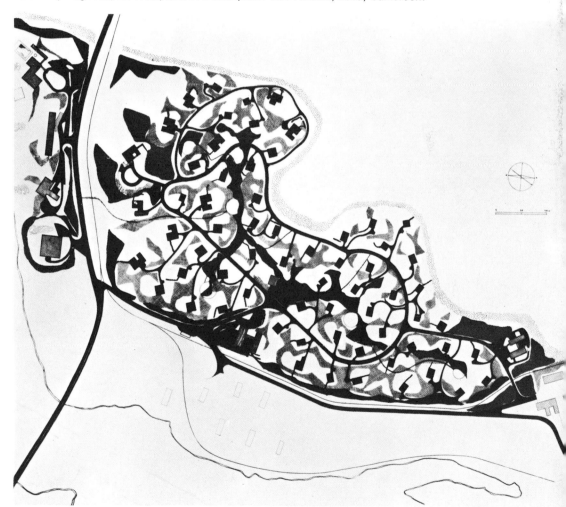

102. *Yona Friedman: Prefabricated houses for the Sahara, project.*

103. *Yona Friedman: Plan for Tunis, Tunisia.*

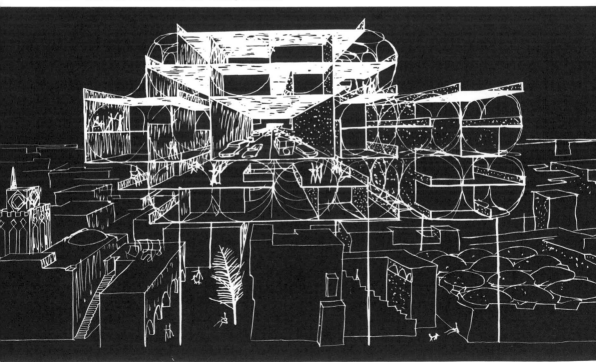

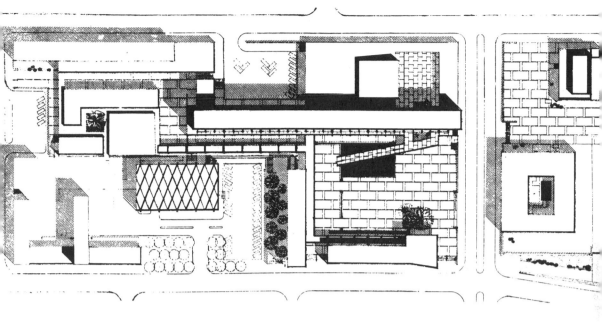

104. (above and below) *Reconstruction of Agadir, Morocco.*

95

TOWARD A NEW
AFRICAN ARCHITECTURE

THE survey of African building tasks and solutions has made it clear that African architecture is only in its beginnings. Here problems have arisen as they rarely have in any other part of the world; they require, above all, the participation of African architects. More precise knowledge and study of the African experience will reveal characteristics which may become common prototypes.

Architectural education in Africa must start from demands which are entirely different from those in Europe or America. John Lloyd, dean of the faculty of architecture at Kumasi University, Ghana (*Figs. 105–106*), saw the principal task in "comprehensive social and environmental design" and proposed four steps: 1) problem-solving as a total discipline; 2) social sciences; 3) physical and environmental science; and 4) structural fabric.

It is evident that architecture in the conventional sense includes only a part of these aspects; in Africa, fundamental conditions which make architecture possible must be treated first. It is essential to evaluate the problems of the African traditional reality correctly, and not to simply transplant solutions which have been developed in Europe or America. More precise study of the African's needs will produce a new methodology surprisingly close to the most advanced theories of Europe or America; for instance, Fumihiko Maki's Group-Form, Oskar Hansen's Open-Form, and other concepts of this type (*Fig. 107*).

It is most important to evaluate Africa's main tasks correctly. These are to make the country fertile, and to promote industrial use of available raw materials. Lloyd has rightly asked: "How many schools of architecture or planning bring the problem of soil fertility before the students?" He comes to the right conclusion: "We have to teach here agriculture, geography, sociology, economics, and a lot of things which no architectural student has to learn in the developed countries."

He uses an analogy to make clear that it is necessary to think in larger terms, in accord with the old but still living African spirit. One should create only outline forms which can be modified in detail by the demands of reality: "We have to construct the trunk and the branches of the tree, and let the leaves be produced by life." New thinking in larger terms, not in preconceived notions, does not produce irreparable fixations which cannot be adapted to later change.

105. *Charles I. Hobbis: School of Architecture, Kumasi University, Ghana, 1960.*

106. *Charles I. Hobbis: School of Architecture, Kumasi University, Ghana. Interior.*

Open forms presuppose that the people who are to live in them share the responsibility (*Fig. 108*): "The 'leaves' can be produced in several ways: marginal improvements can be made to the traditional methods, a better use of traditional materials can be studied, and modern technology can be introduced." What matters is not technology alone, nor the rational revival of local African traditions, but a new element to be gained from these two components. Lloyd confirms this: "What the continent needs is not just technology itself, but the assistance of technology to make a better, more total life." This "total" life, which needs new form and new definition, is the central task. Computers, which, for example, Alan Vaughan-Richards has promoted as tools for the architect, could also play an important part in Africa. In Nigeria alone, six small computers were in operation in 1965. The universities in Lagos and Ibadan have included computer-programming courses in the curriculum.

The conditions for giving outline, shape, and form to the new African personality must be created by Americans and Europeans living in Africa, and by native architects who are only beginning to

107. *Jean-François Zevaco: Regional Tribunal, Beni-Mellal, Morocco, 1964.*

come forward (*Fig. 109*). Both face the same tasks, and the color or race of the architect of a good plan is unimportant. When Amancio d'Alpoim Guedes attacks rational, industrial architecture and writes: "Yet our hunger for buildings as symbols, messages, memorials, chambers of ideas and feelings is so strong that even if their faded medicine has lost the original potency of sign and idea, our need constantly recharges them," he is in accord with a specifically African demand of today. This demand is within the tradition of imaginative Western architecture, not only the architectural imagination of ancient Africa.

We must become technicians of the emotions, tear-jerkers, exaggerators, spokesmen of dreams, performers of miracles, messengers; and invent raw, bold, vigorous and intense buildings without taste, absurd and chaotic—an architecture plugged into people, an architecture the size of life. Our buildings will be artificial organisms, mechanical dolls and monsters, purring and

109. *Elie Azagury: Civic Center, Rabat, Morocco.*

110. *Alan Vaughan-Richards: Vice Chancellor's House, University of Lagos, Nigeria, 1962.*

puffing, blowing and whistling, containing chambers with the muffled roaring of sea-shells, black rooms, lascivious passages, halls of infinitesimal multiplications, visceral houses turned inside out. We must listen to the voices that speak to all of us from the other side of dreams—we must watch for the sights and signs within ourselves so that the archipelago of necessities, ideas, dreams, desires, obsessions will reveal the total function. Building shall yet belong to the people, architecture shall yet become real and alive, and beauty shall yet be warm and convulsive.

Guedes' buildings, for example his Swazie Zimbabwe or his Habitable Woman, link up with both the African and European traditions and attempt a synthesis which fits the physical and psychological climate of Mozambique.

Alan Vaughan-Richards, who arrived at comparable buildings in Nigeria (*Figs. 110–113*), is convinced that solutions by computer are

111. *Alan Vaughan-Richards: Vice Chancellor's Lodge, University of Lagos.*

especially suited to a continuation of the old African tradition: "Africa is the continent which has always used moulded forms, and it could well take the leadership in architecture in the latter part of the century." Only future developments will show whether his forecast is justified.

A contemporary African architecture, which exists only in scattered beginnings, will have to be created by Englishmen and Frenchmen, Belgians and Portuguese, by Berbers schooled in the French tradition, by Yorubas who have studied in England and Switzerland, by Indians in East Africa, and by Kikuyus who have been trained by European architects living in Africa (*Figs. 114–115*). However, more and more young Africans now have the opportunity to acquire the basis for continuing their own tradition, outside Africa in European or American schools of architecture, or in Africa at the technical universities and in offices of British and French architectural firms.

Meanwhile, it would be wishful thinking to judge African architecture only by the achievements of a few native architects. The diversity and complexity of building—the various styles which are side by side and thousands of years apart—have prevented the rise of an indigenous African architecture up to now. But its locally quite

112. *Alan Vaughan-Richards: University of Lagos House, Nigeria, 1962.*

different and modified beginnings are today in Morocco (*Fig. 116*) and Algeria, Nigeria, and Ghana, and in some East African countries like Kenya, Zambia and Uganda, where the new problems are recognized.

Everywhere, European and American architects, who built, planned, or taught in Africa, have made important contributions: Le Corbusier, Walter Gropius, Jørn Utzon, Harry Weese, Ernst May, André Studer, Georges Candilis, Shadrach Woods, Julian Elliott, P. A. Emery, Roland Simounet, E. Maxwell Fry, Jane Drew, Drake and Lasdun, Kenneth Scott, Godwin and Hopwood, Guy Lagneau, Peer Abben, Marcel Mauri, James Cubitt, D. A. Barrett, Norman and Dawbarn, Bernard Zehrfuss, H. Richard Hughes, Peatfield and Bodgener, Aldo van Eyck, Herman Haan, Olaf Jacobsen, Richard Buckminster Fuller, Carsten Schröck, Eckhardt Schulze Fielitz, Amancio d'Alpoim Guedes, and many others. This list shows that the marks of these architects, who have lived and worked in Africa for long or short periods, cannot be erased; their work will be part of the developing architectural tradition of the African continent.

It is necessary to distinguish between architects who know African life and are specialists for the African setting, and those who only

113. *Alan Vaughan-Richards: University of Lagos House.*

114. *Oluwole Olumuyiwa: U.A.C. Housing Development, Lagos, Nigeria. Detail of servants' quarters.*

115. *Olivier-Clement Cacoub: Resort, Skanés, Tunisia, 1966.*

116. *Elie Azagury: Restaurant "Petit Merou," Cabo Negro, Morocco, interior, 1968.*

117. *H. Richard Hughes: Watamu Beach Hotel, near Malindi, Kenya, water tank by artist Jony Waite, 1966.*

worked on an isolated commission. Among the architects who have been active in Africa for decades are Godwin and Hopwood, H. Richard Hughes (*Fig. 117*), Julian Elliott, James Cubitt, Kenneth Scott and E. Maxwell Fry and Jane Drew with their partners Drake and Lasdun: they have determined the image of whole African cities. To this group belong also the Belgian Henri Laurens, who essentially created the cityscape of Leopoldville, the Congo Republic, the Englishman Hughes, and the Dane Peer Abben, who built numerous structures in East African cities. The architects in the French tradition—Chomette, Lagneau, Candilis, and Woods—shaped whole complexes in an African sense; their work is exemplary. Actually, in spite of their long residence in Africa, their solutions are now in the African tradition, and at the same time in the tradition of the French academy—on the one hand, the realization of the conditions under which Africans want to live; on the other, the fixed conception in the style of the French academy, which has nothing to do with the African character.

Architects temporarily active in Africa who have designed individual buildings are Justus Dahinden (a church), Olaf Jacobsen (a school), Walter Gropius (educational buildings), and Harry Weese (an embassy) as well as numerous other builders of embassies in various parts of Africa. Yona Friedman made visionary urbanistic proposals which can be related to ancient African conceptions. Buckminster Fuller held seminars in Lagos and Zarla, and his influence should prove especially important. His universal concepts could lead young Africans to form ideas of their own. Some students conclude that the metal in Fuller's geodesic domes could be replaced by local plant materials.

European and American architects so far outnumber the African architects who have solutions of their own. Almost all of these designers were educated in Europe and America, or by foreign teachers in the young African schools. The results are therefore determined by European or American models. The Moroccan architects Jean-François Zevaco, Elie Azagury and Mourad Ben Embarek come from the French tradition and have built many structures of French-influenced design. In new work, especially Azagury's Civic Center in Rabat, a growing originality can be felt. Other Moroccan architects (such as Mourad Ben Embarek, A. Faroui, and Mohamed Agard) continue the work on the basis created by Azagury.

African architects are also active in Cameroon (N'Sangue), Ivory Coast (Koassy Goly and Aka Adjo), Dahomey (Domingo), Kenya (David Mutiso), and the Malagasy Republic (Razafi Adriamihaingo, Jean Rabemanantsoa, Jean Ratamatanantsoa, and José Ravelomanantsoa). Moreover, in Kenya, the Indian Kersey D. Moddie is represented by various buildings and projects.

The Nigerian architects Olumuyiwa, Ekwueme, and Kola-Bankole, whose country was formerly a British West African colony, were educated in the British tradition. Their buildings are also slowly changing from northern European models. Olumuyiwa knows contemporary Dutch, British, and Swiss architecture (*Fig. 118*); in his school and engineering buildings, his architectural office, and in important new projects, he has made conscious efforts to go back to the old Yoruba tradition (*Figs. 119–120*). His work may be considered typical of the conditions under which an African architect works today; it therefore is instructive to trace his career.

Oluwole Olumuyiwa began his education at the Department of Architecture of the University of Manchester, where he studied from 1949 to 1954; during the last two years he also studied at the Department of City and Regional Planning. In 1954, he received his degree in architecture and city planning—a combination symptomatic of the aims of the younger generation in Africa. After this basic education, Olumuyiwa worked for four years in well known European architec-

118. *André Studer: Apartments, Casablanca, Morocco, 1953–1954.*

tural and city planning offices, first in Britain (Manchester, Stevenage, London), then in Holland in the office of the architects and city planners Van den Broek and Bakema in Rotterdam, and finally in Switzerland, where he was active from 1956 to 1958 in the architectural office of Haefeli, Moser, and Steiger in Zürich. In Rotterdam, he was strongly influenced by the solid, functional Dutch tradition. In Switzerland, he was able to collaborate decisively in the design of hospitals (Cantonal Hospital in Zurich).

In 1958, after nine years of studies, and after travels through nine European and seven African countries, Olumuyiwa returned to his homeland and opened an office in Lagos, where he has now been

119. *Oluwole Olumuyiwa in his Crusaders' House, Lagos, Nigeria, 1968.*

Oluwole Olumuyiwa: College of Engineering, Ibadan, Nigeria, 1963–1964.

active for ten years. His buildings are distinguished by free ground plans and by meaningful use of native materials and methods. Instead of air-conditioning he introduces, especially in his schools, the natural, traditional cross ventilation through "breathing walls." In various cases, he tempers the effect of heat on the roof zone by a built-in air cushion. Beyond his own work, Olumuyiwa takes an active part in all matters concerning the architecture of his country. He is a member of the Nigerian Institute of Architecture, belongs to the examination committee of the Nigerian College of Arts, Science, and Technology in Zaria, and is co-publisher of the country's first architectural magazine, *The West African Builder and Architect*.

Olumuyiwa's buildings are not only distinguished by economy and by the use of the simplest possible native materials but also by strong color contrasts which are rarely found in Europe except in some southern countries. The free ground plan is typical of the new West African architecture; the outdoor space is integrated with the buildings, as in past great African times. Walls and ceilings are designed to protect against sun and rain, but to let the wind through.

The results achieved by the young African architects differ, as do their educational backgrounds. In Morocco the results are different from those in Kenya; in Tunisia, from Nigeria. They also depend on whether the clients are Europeans, Americans, Indians, or Africans. But everywhere, they are marked by inherent, newly discovered African dynamics, by the utmost economy of available means, and by fantasy fed from many sources, often expressed in simple, primitive ways in small objects or inconspicuous details. The common characteristics of these various structures should be furthered by building with one's own hands, by drawing on the imagination of people other than architects, by stressing antirationalism which transcends the rationally possible, and by recognizing that individuality is preserved *within* the mass, not outside the mass. The decisive characteristics of Africa may lie in these directions.

The desert and the jungle, the snow-covered mountains, and the subtropical coasts in the east and south have produced common African constants, in spite of the immense differences and contrasts. They have produced an African personality of today which is unchangeable and distinct from the world's other national personalities. Dance, rhythm, a sense of the body, definite behavior patterns in the community, movement in general, these are typically African attributes, characterizing almost all parts of the continent. These phenomena are rooted in long-buried traditions which must be activated again. The emancipation, the cultural self-respect of the African, is of great importance to today's world situation. It involves the rediscovery of Africa's own heritage. Thus, the great testimony of Zimbabwe and Benin, Luxor and Timbuctoo, Kilwa and Gizeh and cave paintings, with sequences of traditions composed of Bantu, Arabic,

Christian, Indian, and past thought, play a considerable role. They all yield elements of a tradition which is called upon today to make its contribution to world culture. The African tradition, rediscovered after centuries of oblivion—of colonialism with its positive and negative effects, of the technical and industrial revolution which has so abruptly gained a foothold—all merge in a total picture; it is specifically African, rich in nuances and full of contradictions, even polarized in its varied expressions.

Coming generations of African architects will have to give visible expression to this continent, with its boundless, fascinating, dangerous, and provocative possibilities. Africa is in a pioneer period. It will not be able to avoid the vital, brilliant, and destructive times of beginning, in which the pace of development can lead to chaos.

This book attempts only an outline of what has happened with incredible speed since about 1960. The developments force us to await the results of coming years, but it is certain that the achievements of these beginning years will be fundamental for Africa's future. If the development of Africa does not fail, there is hope that these achievements will also impress and enrich the other continents.

BIBLIOGRAPHY

INDEX

SOURCES OF ILLUSTRATIONS

SELECTIVE BIBLIOGRAPHY

Archaeology, Architecture, and Town Planning

Beier, Ulli. "Moderne Architektur in Nigerien," *Baukunst und Werkform* (1957).

Beinart, Julian. "Come sarà l'architettura in Africa," *Edilizia Moderna*, 89/90, (1967).

Cantacuzino, Sherban. "The Work of James Cubitt and Partners," *Architecture and Building* (April, 1957).

Fraser, Douglas. *Village Planning in the Primitive World.* New York, 1968.

Fry, E. Maxwell. "Town Planning in West Africa," *Architects' Year Book 2.* London, 1947.

————, and Drew, Jane. *Tropical Architecture.* New York, 1956; rev. ed., 1964.

————. *Village Housing in the Tropics.* London, 1953.

Haan, Herman, "Matmata," in *The Pedestrian and The City,* ed. David Lewis. London, 1965.

Hall, R. N. *Ancient Ruins of Rhodesia.* 1904.

————. *Great Simbabwe.* 1905.

Hensen, J. "Architecture et Urbanisme du Maroc," *A + U, Architecture et Urbanisme,* 5 (1967).

Hicks, D. T. "Rebuilt Agadir," *The Architectural Review* (October, 1967).

Hirschfelder, G. "Wohnungsbau in Sansibar," *Deutsche Architektur,* 9 (1964).

Howie, W. D. *Contemporary Architecture in South Africa.* Johannesburg, 1958.

Kultermann, Udo. "Afrikaner bauen für Afrikaner," *Die Tat* (September 28, 1967).

————. "Architettura di africani per africani," *Casabella,* 306, (1966).

————. "Comment construisent les jeunes Africaines," *Afrique* (November, 1962).

————. "Die neue Architektur in Afrika" *Kölnische Rundschan* (1960).

————. "In einem panz anderen Land," *Die Kunst au Hause in Sein.* Munich, 1965.

————. *Neues Bauen in Afrika.* Tübingen, 1963. (*New Architecture in Africa.* New York, 1963).

————. "Schaut auf Simbabwe," *Artis,* 4, (1966).

————. "Wie bauen die jungen Afrikanev," *Tagesspiegel* (1961).

Mas, P. "Ordinamento del territorio in Africa," *Casabella,* 300 (1965).

McConnell, R. S. "Assuam. Egypt's Third City, *Architectural Review* (August, 1966).

Okin, Theophilus Adelodun. *The Urbanized Nigerian.* New York, 1968.

Pedrals, Denis Pierre de. *Archéologie de l'Afrique noire.* Paris, 1950.

Richards, J. M. *New Building in the Commonwealth.* London, 1961.

Vaughan-Richards, A. "The New Generation," *The West African Builder and Architect* (March/April, 1967).

————. "Future Architectural Design," *Nigeria* (1967).

Waugh, Edward and Elizabeth. *The South Builds: New Architecture in the Old South.* Chapel Hill, 1960.

Art

Adam, Leonhard. *Primitive Art*. Harmondsworth, Middlesex, 1949.

Bockstedte, W. "Kunststoffe in Afrika," *Neues Afrika* V (1963).

Diop, A. *L'Art Nègre*. 1951.

Fagg, William. *Tribes and Forms in African Art*. New York, 1965.

————, and Delanae, J. *African Art*. New York, 1968.

————, and Eliot Elisofon. *The Sculpture of Africa*. London and New York, 1958.

————, and Margaret Plass. *African Sculpture: An Anthology*. London and New York, 1964.

Forman, W. *Kunst von Benin*. Prague, 1960.

Hardy, Georges. *L'Art Nègre*. Paris, 1927.

Herskovits, Melville J. *Background of African Art*. Denver, 1945.

Himmelheber, Hans. *Negerkunst und Negerkünstler*. Braunschweig, 1960.

————. *Negerkünstler*. Stuttgart, 1935.

Leiris, Michel. *L'Afrique fantôme*. Paris, 1934.

Leuzinger, Elsy. *Afrika—Kunst der Welt*. Baden-Baden, 1959. (*Africa: The Art of the Negro Peoples*. Art of the World. New York, 1960).

Rachewiltz, Boris de. *Afrikanische Kunst*. Zurich, 1960.

Schmalenbach, Werner. *Die Kunst Afrikas*. Basel, 1953.

Sydow, Eckart von: *Handbuch der westafrikanischen Plastik*. Berlin, 1930.

Theile, Albert. *Kunst in Afrika*. Stuttgart, 1961.

Wassing, R. S. *African Art and Traditions*. New York, 1968.

Economic, Political, and Social Background

Ansprenger, Franz. *Politik im Schwarzen Afrika*. Cologne, 1961.

Aujoulat, Louis-Paul. *Aujourd'hui, l'Afrique*. Tournai, 1960.

Azikiwe, Nnamdi. *Economic Reconstruction of Nigeria*. 1943.

————. *Liberia in World Politics*. London, 1934.

————. *Renascent Africa*. Accra, 1937.

Balandier, Georges. *Zwielichtiges Afrika*. Stuttgart, 1959.

Barenne, Y. *La modernisation rurale au Maroc*. Paris, 1948.

Bascom, William R., and Herskovits, Melville J. *Continuity and Change in African Cultures*. Chicago, 1959.

Biobaku, Sabari Olademi. "Entwicklungspolitik und afrikanischer Sozialismus," *Neues Afrika*, V (1963).

Bonn, Gisela. *Neue Welt am Nil*. Wiesbaden, 1953.

Bourgiba, Habib. *La Tunesie et la France*. Paris, 1954.

Bühlmann, Walbert. *Afrika—gestern, heute, morgen*. Freiburg, 1961.

Calder, Ritchie. *Prüfstein des Weissen Mannes*. Düsseldorf, 1961.

Cameron, James. *Die afrikanische Revolution*. Cologne, 1961. (*The African Revolution*. London, 1961).

Campbell, Alexander. *The Heart of Africa*. New York, 1954.

Caton-Thompson, G. *The Zimbabwe Culture*, Oxford, 1931.

Catz, Paul. *Afrika straks*. Amsterdam, 1947.

Célesier, C. *Le Maroc*. Paris, 1948.

Cerulli, Enrico. *Somalia*, I–II. Rome, 1957.

Cornet, René J. *Katanga*. Brussels, 1946.

Davidson, Basil. *The African Awakening*. 1954.

————. *Report on Southern Africa*. 1952.

Decraene, Philippe. *Le Panafricanisme*. Paris, 1959.

Delafosse, Maurice. *Les Nègres*. Paris, 1927.

Dia, Mamadou. *L'Économique africainé*. Paris, 1957.

————. *Nations africaines et solidarite mondiale*. Paris, 1960.

Dubois, W. E. B. *The World and Africa*. New York, 1947.

Dugué, Gil. *Vers les États-Unis d'Afrique*. Dakar, 1960.

Elsing, J. M. *Sikelela Afrika*. Zürich, 1961.

Filesi, Teobaldo. *Communismo e nazionalismo in Africa*. Rome, 1958.

Gorer, G. *Geheimes Afrika*. Bern, 1950.

Hailey, W. M. *An African Survey*. London, 1957.

Illner, Hans Peter. *Afrika in der Entwicklung*. Braunschweig, 1964.

Italiaander, Rolf. *Schwarze Haut im roten Griff*. Düsseldorf, 1961.

————. *Nordafrika heute*. Hamburg, 1954.

Jahn, Janheinz. *Durch afrikanische Türen*. Düsseldorf, 1960.

Jenny, Hans. *Afrika ist nicht nur schwarz*. Düsseldorf, 1961.

Kaufmann, Herbert. *Nigeria*. Bonn, 1958.

————. *Afrikas Weg in die Gegenwart*. Braunschweig, 1963.

Klages, J. *Navrongo*. Zürich, 1953.

Kleist, Peter. *Südafrika*. Göttingen, 1963.

Léger, Jean. *Afrique française—Afrique nouvelle*. Ottawa, 1958.

Lumumba, Patrice. *Le Congo—terre d'avenir—est-il menace?* Brussels, 1961.

Luschan, Felix von. *Altertümer von Benin*. Berlin, 1919.

Maquet, Jacques Jérome. "Schwarz-Afrika im Zeitalter der Industrialisierung," *Neues Afrika*, V (1963).

Marvel, Tom. *The New Congo*. New York, 1948.

Mboya, Tom. *The Kenya Question: An African Answer*. London, 1956.

Merle Davis, J. *Modern Industry and the African*. London, 1933.

Mukarovsky, Hans. *Afrika. Geschichte und Gegenwart*. Vienna, 1961.

Nkrumah, Kwame. *Education and Nationalism in West Africa*. 1943.

————. *Ghana. Autobiography of Kwame Nkrumah*. 1957.

————. *Toward Colonial Freedom*. 1946.

————. *What I Mean by Positive Action*. 1950.

Otto, Eberhard. *Agypten*. Stuttgart, 1961.

Pankhurst, Estelle Sylvia. *Education in Ethiopia*. Woodford, 1946.

Plum, Werner. *Nordafrika*. Nuremburg, 1961.

Reichhold, W. *Westafrika*. Bonn, 1958.

Richter, L. *Inseln der Sahara*. Leipzig, 1960. (*Islands of the Sahara: Through the Oases of Libya*. Leipzig, 1960.)

Rifaat Bey, Mohammed. *The Awakening of Modern Egypt*. London, 1948.

Rohrbach, Paul. *Afrika heute und morgen*. Berlin, 1939.

Schatten, Fritz. *Afrika—schwarz oder rot?* Munich, 1961.

Schulthess, E. *Afrika*. Zürich, 1958, 1959.

Scott, Michael. *A Time to Speak*. London, 1958.

————. *Attitude to Africa*. 1951.

————. *Shadow over Africa*. London, 1950.

Sirvex, Paul. *Une Nouvelle Afrique*. Paris, 1957.

Sithole, Ndabaningi. *African Nationalism*. London and New York, 1959.

Suret-Canale, Jean. *Afrique Noire*. Paris, 1958.

Verg, E. *Das Afrika der Afrikaner*. Stuttgart, 1960.

Weisgerber, F. *Au seuil du Maroc moderne*. Rabat, 1947.

Wilson, Charles M. *Liberia*. New York, 1947.

Zischka, Anton. *Abessinien*. Leipzig, 1935.

————. *Afrika. Europas Gemeinschaftsaufgabe*. Oldenburg, 1951.

Historical, Anthropological, and Cultural Studies

Alimen, Henriette. *Préhistoire de l'Afrique*. Paris, 1955.

Baumann, Hermann and Westermann, Diedrich. *Les Peuples et les civilizations de l'Afrique*. Paris, 1948.

Busia, Kofi Abrefa. *The Ashanti*. London, 1954.

Davidson, Basil. *Urzeit und Geschichte Afrikas*. Hamburg, 1961.

Diop, A. *Schwarze Völker und Kultur*. Paris, 1954.

Egharevba, Jacob U. *A Short History of Benin*. Benin, 1953.

Frobenius, Leo. *Das Unbekannte Afrika*. Munich, 1923.

————. *Im Schatten des Kongostaates*. Berlin, 1907.

————. *Kulturgeschichte Afrikas*. Zürich, 1933.

————. *Und Afrika sprach*. . . . Berlin, 1912.

German, P. *Die Grundlagen der afrikanischen Kultur*. Leipzig, 1948.

Gibbs, Henry. *Twilight in South Africa*. New York, 1950.

Hassert, Kurt. *Die Erforschung Afrikas*. Leipzig, 1942.

Herskovits, Melville J. *Acculturation*. 1938.

————. *The Myth of the Negro Past*. 1941.

Jahn, Janheinz. *Durch afrikanische Türne*. Düsseldorf, 1960.

Jensen, Adolf Ellegard. *Im Lande des Gada*. Stuttgart, 1936.

Krige, E. J. *The Social System of the Zulus*. London. 1936.

Lévi-Strauss, Claude. *Tristes tropiques*. Paris, 1955.

Luschan, Felix von. *Altertümer von Benin*. Berlin, 1919.

Murdock, George P. *Africa: Its People and Their Cultural History*. New York, 1959.

Roth, H. L. *Great Benin*. Halifax, 1903.

Tempels, Placide. *Bantuphilosophie*. Heidelberg, 1956.

Walton, James. *African Village*. Pretoria, 1956.

Westermann, Diedrich. *Geschichte Afrikas*. Cologne, 1952.

INDEX

SOURCES OF ILLUSTRATIONS

1. Direction du Tourisme, Tunis, Tunisia.
2. David Lewis (ed.), *The Pedestrian and the City*, Elek Books, London, 1965, p. 126.
3–4. Douglas Fraser, *Village Planning in the Primitive World*, George Braziller, Inc., New York, 1968, Figs. 58–59.
5. E. Maxwell Fry and Jane Drew, *Tropical Architecture*, B. T. Batsford, Ltd., London, 1964, p. 136.
6–10. Udo Kultermann, Leverkusen, Germany.
11. Peter Pitt, London, England.
12. A. Ifeanyi Ekwueme, Lagos, Nigeria.
13. Oluwole Olumuyiwa, Lagos, Nigeria.
14. S. I. Kola-Bankole, Lagos, Nigeria.
15–16. G. Gherardi-A. Fiorelli, Rome, Italy.
17. Julian Elliott, Capetown, Republic of South Africa.
18. Opticam, Tananarive, the Malagasy Republic.
19. Peter Pitt, London, England.
20. Marc Lacroix, Casablanca, Morocco.
21. Udo Kultermann, *New Architecture in Africa*, Universe Books, New York, 1963, p. 92.
22. John Godwin and Gillian Hopwood, Lagos, Nigeria.
23. Dotun Okubanjo, Lagos, Nigeria.
24–25. Udo Kultermann, Leverkusen, Germany.
26–27. Marc Lacroix, Casablanca, Morocco.
28. Jean-François Zevaco, Casablanca, Morocco.
29. Marc Lacroix, Casablanca, Morocco.
30. Jean-François Zevaco, Casablanca, Morocco.
31. Opticam, Tananarive, the Malagasy Republic.
32. Andrault and Parat, Paris, France.
33–36. Marc Lacroix, Casablanca, Morocco.
37. Lucien Fargeot, Casablanca, Morocco.
38. Udo Kultermann, *New Architecture in Africa*, Universe Books, New York, 1963, p. 7.
39–42. Elie Azagury, Casablanca, Morocco.
43. Jean-François Zevaco, Casablanca, Morocco.
44. Dotun Okubanjo, Lagos, Nigeria.
45. H. Richard Hughes, Nairobi, Kenya.
46. Studio Charlejan, Brazzaville, the Congo Republic.
47. Lucien Fargeot, Casablanca, Morocco.
48. Marc Lacroix, Casablanca, Morocco.
49. Dotun Okubanjo, Lagos, Nigeria.
50. Van Raenpenbusch, Tunis, Tunisia.
51–52. Udo Kultermann, *New Architecture in Africa*, Universe Books, New York, 1963, pp. 62, 63.
53. Giulia Veronesi and Bruno Alfieri (eds.), *Lotus: Architectural Annual, 1965–1966*, Bruno Alfieri and Editoriale Metro, Milan, 1965, p. 47.

54. Udo Kultermann, *New Architecture in Africa*, Universe Books, New York, 1963, p. 68.

55. Dotun Okubanjo, Lagos, Nigeria.

56. H. Richard Hughes, Nairobi, Kenya.

57. Udo Kultermann, *New Architecture in Africa*, Universe Books, New York, 1963, p. 52.

58. John Godwin and Gillian Hopwood, Lagos, Nigeria.

59. Marc and Evelyn Bernheim, New York City.

60. H. Richard Hughes, Nairobi, Kenya.

61–62. Patrice Guichard, Tunis, Tunisia.

63–64. Elie Azagury, Casablanca, Morocco.

65. Marc Lacroix, Casablanca, Morocco.

66. Dotun Okubanjo, Lagos, Nigeria.

67–69. Udo Kultermann, *New Architecture in Africa*, Universe Books, New York, 1963, pp. 39, 41, 42.

70. Marc Lacroix, Casablanca, Morocco.

71, 73. Udo Kultermann, *New Architecture in Africa*, Universe Books, New York, 1963, pp. 140, 127.

72. Fry, Drew, Drake, and Lasdun, London, England.

74–75, 77. Udo Kultermann, *New Architecture in Africa*, Universe Books, New York, 1963, pp. 133, 134, 136.

76. Julian Elliott, Ndola, Zambia.

78. Willie Bell.

79–81. Elie Azagury, Casablanca, Morocco.

82–83. E. Maxwell Fry and Jane Drew, *Tropical Architecture*. B. T. Batsford, Ltd., London, 1964, pp. 69, 115.

84. Udo Kultermann, *New Architecture in Africa*, Universe Books, New York, 1963, p. 149.

85–88. D.P.C., Accra, Ghana.

89–90. Julian Elliott, Capetown, South Africa.

91–93. Roland Simounet.

94–95. Opticam, Tananarive, the Malagasy Republic.

96. Elie Azagury, Casablanca, Morocco.

97. Marcel J. Mauri, Oran, Algeria.

98. André Studer, Zürich, Switzerland.

99. Elie Azagury, Casablanca, Morocco.

100–101. Udo Kultermann, *New Architecture in Africa*, Universe Books, New York, 1963, pp. 178, 179.

102–103. Udo Kultermann, *New Architecture in Africa*, Universe Books, New York, 1963, pp. 149, 180.

104. *Architectural Review* (October, 1967), pp. 294, 296.

105–106. Charles I. Hobbis, London.

107. Jean-François Zevaco, Casablanca, Morocco.

108–109. Elie Azagury, Casablanca, Morocco.

110–113. Alan Vaughan-Richards, Lagos, Nigeria.

114. Dotun Okubanjo, Lagos, Nigeria.

115. Patrice Guichard, Tunis, Tunisia.

116. Elie Azagury, Casablanca, Morocco.

117. H. Richard Hughes, Nairobi, Kenya.

118. André Studer, Zürich, Switzerland.

119. Oluwole Olumuyiwa, Lagos, Nigeria.

120. Dotun Okubanjo, Lagos, Nigeria.